THE
STORY ⚙ WORKS
Guide to Writing
CHARACTER

Alida Winternheimer

This is a 28.5press book.

1. Fiction—Writing. 2. Fiction—Character. 3. Fiction—Craft. I.Title.

ISBN: 978-0-9912923-9-4

Cover design by Daria Brennan.
Interior design by Jana Rade.
Edited by Dara Syrkin.

for my teachers
past, present, and future

Get Your Bonus

Thank you for picking up *The Story Works Guide to Writing Character.*

Please visit www.WordEssential.com/JoinStoryWorks.

You'll receive a downloadable, fillable Agency Tree worksheet, with instructions and a new example, to help you keep your characters in the game. To learn more about the Agency Tree, see chapter 6.

You'll also:

- receive Alida's newsletter with videos of writing tips,
- be notified when future books in The Story Works Guide to Writing Fiction Series come out,
- be the first to hear about writing courses, and
- get special offers.

Don't forget the cool factor!

Inspiration usually comes during
work, rather than before it.

~ Madeleine L'Engle

Contents

Foreword

Writers walk one of the most difficult paths, because it is largely self-guided. We read books like this one, not because some school is demanding it, but because we'll do anything to further our craft.

A whole sea of craft books is available to us. Which one do we choose? What topic do we start with? Plot? Setting? Viewpoint? As a novice writer, the answer wasn't clear to me, so I read them all. (Spoiler: the answer is character.)

In October of 2014, I published my first novel. To my immense surprise, *No Such Thing As Werewolves* was well received. People really liked it, but I had no idea why. What was my secret ingredient? I wasn't sure if I could replicate "it" for the sequel.

I went looking for answers. I asked other authors, and they told me I needed a writing coach.

I didn't even realize such a thing existed, but the instant I heard the term, I knew a good coach would be invaluable.

My search led me to Alida Winternheimer, a soft-spoken woman who will bluntly tell you all about your weaknesses. I love her for that. She's a writer's best friend.

Alida explained to me exactly why my first novel had succeeded. It was the characters. I'd based every one of my characters on someone I knew. They had flaws, and that came out on the page. My characters felt real, because they were.

Over the course of the next three novels, Alida taught me how to achieve deliberately what I'd done accidentally. She taught me to deepen my characters and how to give them motivation. Most important, she taught me to create conflict between them.

No Mere Zombie and *Vampires Don't Sparkle* are fan favorites. Those were the first two books Alida edited for me, and many of the moments fans loved were born out of her tutelage. Suddenly, my nicey-nice characters transformed into human beings, and readers couldn't put my books down.

Great characters are the core of a great novel. They are the foundation everything else is built on. I will forever be grateful to Alida for teaching me that.

Chris Fox
Novato, California
July 18, 2016

Introduction

Why It's so Hard to Write a Good Character

Characters define a story, give it life and breath, bring readers to the page and keep them reading long after they should have gone to sleep.

As a writer, I want to create a character that acts and feels real, with genuine emotions and feelings. I want that rewarding experience of writing a character that has taken the reins of my story and is directing the words on the page. I want to create a character that grabs readers with both hands and leads them through the story.

But what I want (as with so many things in life) is easier said than done.

If I don't spend enough time with my character before writing my story, I find myself faced with the daunting task of backfilling the details. Or even changing my character to make the story work. Or changing the story to fit my character. As someone who adores the

3

organizational high of an outline, this attempt to fix things after I'm partway through my first draft makes me crazy.

My stories always start with a character. I usually get a snippet of a voice, a personality, posture, or a scene with a certain feel or attitude to it. Once I have that germ of an idea, I can start manipulating it in my head, moving these new infantile beings through various situations until I get a good idea of who they are. Then I get to start building a story around them.

With that first tiny piece of the story twirling around in my mind, the hard work begins. After writing numerous stories with characters that struggle to hold together, or seem to stagnate somewhere around the middle, I've identified a few common problems that I face in my writing.

I tend toward creating perfect people for the situations I am placing them in. Instead of struggling and growing, my characters seem destined to succeed—and breezily. Failure simply isn't an option. And they always make the right choices to avoid consequences. They need to be a peacemaker? Turns out they've got six years of experience in the police force as a negotiator. They need to win a fight? They were a soldier for the last decade. Need to disable a bomb? Electrical engineer. Battle goblins? They studied under that one knight—didn't they? Whatever situation I put my characters in, they seem to have the answer, and I have to go back, rework my characters, take away their proficiencies, or fix it so their perfect solutions don't make perfect results.

Sometimes, I run headlong into my story without taking a hard look at why my characters are in this story to begin with. They have no vested interest in this problem and no motivation to fix it. My characters struggle to participate, and when I try to manipulate them into the story I want, they come across as whiny or complacent. I've forgotten to give my characters the passion and motivation they need. They don't want to stand up to authority, save the world, or even run away from home. In fact, they are more than content to let anyone else handle the problem.

I've met writers who don't struggle with their characters' flaws or motivation. Their characters have some serious sins in their backstory, and they have every reason to be out there battling their demons. But these writers put too much on the page. The story is bloated with explanations of why their characters are who they are without actually moving the story forward.

What about those writers who put all of their effort into their protagonists and forget to invest any time or thought into their antagonists? Or they create the perfect protagonist and antagonist, who have just the right balance of everything, but all of the supporting characters are flat, cardboard stereotypes? Or everyone surrounding the protagonist serves the exact same purpose, a squad of cheerleaders who have no stories of their own?

It is so much easier said than done. Sometimes, I don't know my character isn't working. Other times, I can tell he's not working for me, but I'm not sure what exactly is wrong. And still other times, I know what's wrong with my character, but I don't know how to fix him. As a writer, I struggle with character because crafting a character is an extended and difficult process. It is something that requires care and attention at every step of the story (and let's all admit that sometimes, after the first few shiny chapters, our characters become stubborn and frustrating).

But what does it look like when a writer creates amazing characters, engaging and delightful characters who drive the plot and grow through the story? Those characters grab the readers' attention so that they sympathize with, care for, and love or hate the character, but always they want to read more.

In the end, we all want to create that amazing character that captures readers and won't let go. Writing the perfect character is a process. Investing the time to hone our character-developing skills is the most important thing we can do as writers. And our characters deserve our time and attention long before we put words on a page.

That is what we are here for, and we came to the right place. Congratulations, writers, our journey to crafting amazing characters starts right now!

Kathryn Arnold
Seattle, Washington
August 6, 2016

Chapter 1

How to Use This Book

A NOTE FROM ALIDA

Thank you for picking up *The Story Works Guide to Writing Character*. I know there are a lot of craft books out there, a sea of them, according to Chris Fox. I appreciate that you've chosen my book with the expectation that you'll learn about creating dynamic characters that speak to your readers.

You, like other writers I work with, have a dream to not only publish a book, but to publish a really *good* book, and to go on publishing really good books. Those are the kind of books that turn readers into fans. And you know that success as a writer is not about production schedules or professional covers. Those things are critical components of the publishing business, but every book begins as words on the page. Those words are your story. Your readers are after a good story. And your story begins and ends with your main character.

Whether you know it or not, you have a social contract with your reader: you, as the author, must create a main character worth your reader's time and energy, not to mention money. Do so, and she will gladly spend her leisure time with your story, savoring every moment. When you create a character your reader falls in love with, she'll come back for the next book in the series. She'll become your fan. She'll talk about your characters like they're real people—the way you do.

You are a dedicated writer, eager to learn and willing to work toward your goal. You also enjoy the process of creating a story. You can geek out about story craft and crack up over how ridiculously much fun it is to build an entire universe from nothing. I hope you enjoy reading this book as much as I have enjoyed writing it.

WHAT YOU'LL GET FROM THIS BOOK

In these pages, you'll find exercises with steps you can apply to your writing that will change how you approach character. These exercises work for whatever character you're developing right now, however far into that development you are. You can repeat these exercises every time you create a new character. Nothing is abstract. Everything applies to every character you create, however high or low on your character pyramid. You'll create characters your readers miss between books. You'll discover the vital connection between your characters and subplots. You'll see theme in a new light. You'll learn how to *know* if your character is an active protagonist. And you'll find many excerpts that provide practical examples to study and compare.

I designed this book to be an ongoing resource, something you can keep within reach and come back to whenever you get stuck. At the end of each chapter is a Recap section you can use as quick reference material. The final chapter is titled "Problems with Character (And How to Fix Them)" and is another quick reference tool for when you need that one specific solution to your character problem. At the back of the book, you'll find a glossary of key terms with page numbers for further reference. Each term in the glossary is italicized when it is first defined in the text. You'll also find a list of the thirteen exercises in this book and their locations.

Story is comprised of character, plot, and setting. It's impossible to isolate one aspect of story from the others. They're like the three strands of a braid, woven together to create a whole. I mention plot and setting throughout this book, because there are times when the only way to understand how your character functions in your story is to consider the other strands of the narrative braid.

THE EXAMPLES IN THIS BOOK

I will often use examples from my own work. That's because I can both analyze them and explain my choices as the writer. Also, I own the material, so there's no concern with copyright.

A good number of my editing and coaching clients have given me permission to use their work as examples in this series of books. When you see an excerpt that is not from my work, it's from one of these brave writers. I am finding it easy to use positive examples, but these writers gave their permission with the understanding that I might excerpt a work in progress to point out what not to do, and I am indebted to them for their trust. There are links at the back of the book so you can find their work. Please do!

Throughout this book, I'm going to discuss your main, or point of view, character in the singular, as though the character is a human being. It is understood that you might have multiple point of view characters. It is also understood that your character might not be human.

I am going to talk about rules of story craft and what you should or should not do. I gladly acknowledge that there are exceptions to every rule and circumstances where bending the rule is the best thing you could do. Exceptions and rule bending must be examined on a case-by-case basis, which is beyond the scope of this book. I will, however, point out some of the most common exceptions to the rules.

THE CREATIVE POWER OF PREWRITING BY HAND

If you search "handwriting and creativity" online, you'll find plenty of articles about the benefits of handwriting and concern over its disappearance from our culture and elementary curriculums. One study by Virginia Berninger, a psychologist at the University of Washington, demonstrated that printing, cursive writing, and typing on a keyboard are all associated with distinct and separate brain patterns. When subjects composed text by hand, they consistently produced more words and expressed more ideas. Brain imaging suggested that the connection between writing and idea generation went even further. The subjects with better handwriting exhibited greater neural activation in areas associated with working memory and increased overall activation in the reading and writing networks (Konnikova, Maria. "What's Lost as Handwriting Fades." *New York Times,* June 2, 2014). There is also plenty of anecdotal evidence from writers to be found in conversations, interviews, blogs, etc., professing that grabbing a pen is often critical to the creative process, whether that's generating a first draft or stepping away from the keyboard to get unstuck. You don't have to believe me or the research. Get a journal for the exercises in this book. As you do them, exercise your fine motor control by putting pen to paper—and watch your creativity get a boost!

SKILLS AND CONFIDENCE

You will come away from reading this book with a strong sense of the importance of character, an understanding of what it takes to build a believable character, and the skills to do so with confidence.

The Story Works Guide to Writing Fiction Series exists to help you write better stories, for yourself, for your stories, for your readers.

May you grow as a storyteller, and may your readers fall in love with your characters.

Chapter 2

The Heart of Your Story

A WELL-DEFINED CHARACTER

Stories are built around characters, and your *main character* is the heart of your story. Readers connect to that heart. Without it, you don't have a story; you have a series of events. When the Hindenburg went down in flames on May 6, 1937, the radio journalist Herbert Morrison cried, "Oh, the humanity!"

> However dramatic a spectacle you create, it cannot deeply move your reader unless you involve characters the reader cares about.

WWWWW + H

You've probably heard of the five Ws plus the H of journalism: who, what, when, where, why, and how. They are—I have heard—fundamental to journalism. They are also fundamental to storytelling. You need to address each of them, and your reader needs to have a sense of them in order to engage with your story.

Character is about the who and the why. Who is this story about? Why is this person the center of this particular story? Why does this person make the choices she makes and do what she does?

Let's look at the who. Say we're writing a story about Jane, an heir to the throne who doesn't know she's the heir to the throne. Jane is young, pretty, well mannered, naive, and more special than she knows.

Why is Jane the center of this particular story? This part of why has to do with your scenario. It answers for the specialness of your main character. No other character could fill this role. In this case, the scenario that makes Jane special is that she's unknowingly the heir to the throne. A lot of things will now happen to Jane *because* she is the heir, like villains trying to prevent her ascension to the throne.

The other part of why has to do with character motivation. It addresses the choices Jane makes and the actions she takes. It's about nature and nurture. Nature: if Jane is shy and lacking inner strength, she'll respond to threats differently than if she is a natural-born badass. Nurture: if Jane has been raised by peasant farmers, she'll have different skills than if she has been raised by Shaolin kung fu masters.

We'll discuss the what of plot and the when and where of setting in the other books in this series.

CHARACTER DEFINED

Character is two things:

First, character is the vehicle through which a reader engages with a story.

We may pick up a story because it has a lot of car crashes or a lot of kissing, but we remember a story because we care about the people involved in the crashes or doing the kissing. That's because human beings are hardwired to *empathize* with each other. What this means for you is that your main character has to be likable and fascinating enough that a reader will engage with him for the duration of the story, whether that's a ten-page short story, three-hundred-page novel, or eight-hundred-page series. Readers attach themselves to the *point of view (POV) character*. The point of view character provides the perspective through which the reader experiences the story. Readers empathize deeply with the point of view character, forming a heart to heart connection. That might sound sappy, but it's true. If your reader doesn't care deeply for your main character, your book *is* forgettable.

Second, character is any conscious being who acts in a story and changes over time.

Every character must have consciousness, an awareness of the world in which she exists. A character must also act, that is she must have *agency,* a means by which to choose what to do when, where, with whom, and to whom.

The protagonist and title character in Shel Silverstein's *The Giving Tree* is rooted to the spot, but is completely aware of her world and has agency. She shapes her own fate, falling in love with a little boy and then giving of herself (literally) until all that remains of her is a stump. For a character who can't even move, she exemplifies agency. By choosing what to give to the boy and when, she acts and changes over time.

Your character must change over time. To be a well-developed, complex, compelling protagonist, your character must have an *arc*, an internal change brought about by the events of the story. Why? Because every story is a journey.

BEGIN AT THE BEGINNING

Your story needs a compelling character or no one will want to read it. How are you going to create a character who inspires enduring loyalty? A long series with loving fans? A movie deal? Action figures? I get ahead of myself. Let's come back to where it all begins. Right here. With a paper and pencil.

There is a kinesthetic experience that occurs when you write longhand. Although it's slower than typing, it's worth it. All of my books begin with a journal where I keep notes about the characters and plot *development*. The prewriting begins long before I draft any of the story and continues until the book is finished.

Have you ever started a simple plumbing project around the house—on a Sunday evening, naturally—and found fifteen minutes into it that you need a wrench you don't own? So you run to the hardware store and buy one. You come home and get the fixture opened up, to find the O ring is dry and cracked. You run back to the hardware store. You get there right before they close and buy the new O ring. You go home and think you're all set, only to discover that the real problem is inside the wall. And the hardware store just closed. And now your sink is pulled apart. And you have to go to work in the morning. That's what it's like to try to write a book when you haven't done your prewriting. At every turn, you find yourself confronting some new problem, some direction that dead-ends, some character you can't figure out. Developing your characters before you begin writing will save you time and frustration later.

> Your characters aren't flung fully formed into the midst of your story. They need development, and that begins with your prewriting.

Throughout this book, you'll learn how to develop your characters. Grab your journal and pencil, and let's begin now.

EXERCISE 1: THE GREAT CHARACTER

In this exercise, we're going to explore what makes a character memorable and make sure your characters actually demonstrate the qualities you assign them.

Note: I recommend you get a notebook or journal and use it for all of the exercises in this book, doing each one as you encounter it. At the end of the process, you'll have created a manual for your character that you can use to ensure continuity throughout your book or series.

1. Think of a favorite character you've encountered in literature. Don't worry about whether anyone would agree with you or not, just pick a character you love from a book you've read.

2. Make a list of everything you remember about this character's traits, her personality and features. Keep going. Make it a long list.

3. Write down how you feel about this character. Why do you like her so much? What makes her so memorable? Dig down.

4. Does the character seem like a real person to you?

5. Compare how you feel about the character to the list of traits and things that make her memorable. Think about how the author portrayed this character to create a real-seeming person.

6. Remove or replace some of those memorable traits with their opposites. For example, Atticus Finch of Harper Lee's *To Kill a Mockingbird* is gentle and considerate. What if he has a temper? How would the character, the story, and your feelings change?

The list you just made should give you an idea of what goes into making a character that readers will connect with. A common issue with portraying characters is that writers might really know the character, but don't get all that knowledge on the page for the reader. By examining someone else's character, you have to rely on what is on the page—not what is in your head—which is what makes this exercise so useful.

As you work with your own character now, try to put yourself in your reader's head. To help you do this, grab a highlighter and something you've written. Anything will do, even if you retired it to "the round file cabinet."

7. Think of one of your own characters. Ask yourself how a reader, a perfect stranger who has never seen the inside of your head, would answer these same questions about your character. Write out how you believe a reader will see your character.

8. Since your reader can't get inside your head, print out a few scenes and read them with a highlighter. Highlight everywhere your character's traits are shown on the page. If you've listed the trait "clumsy," highlight the words that describe her tripping over her own feet. If you describe her as an "animal lover," highlight the words that describe her rescuing a mutt from a shelter. Whatever you think makes your character lifelike and memorable, make sure you've highlighted the evidence to support those claims.

9. If you can't highlight the evidence that illustrates the traits you've assigned to your character, it's not on the page and you *cannot* count it as an identifiable trait. You'd better change your opinion of your character or rewrite some scenes.

Your reader is not inside your head. He will judge your characters solely based on the words you put on the page.

If you are ever in doubt about how well you're portraying your character, or if you get feedback from workshops or advance readers that your characters are other than you believe them to be, come back to this exercise. Make a list of your character's traits. Then read your manuscript with a highlighter and find the evidence that shows the character to be who you think he is. Revise as necessary.

RECAP

Note: Each Recap section contains a bulleted list of the chapter's main points, so that you can use it as a quick reference guide to the chapter later, when you're looking for that specific piece of the discussion.

In this chapter, we've defined character and begun the prewriting work that develops a character.

- Character is the heart of story.
- Readers will return to a series because of the characters, not the action.
- Your character is the vehicle through which readers engage with your story.
- Character is any conscious being who acts in a story and changes over time.
- Prewriting before you begin drafting your manuscript will save you frustration later.
- Make sure the traits you believe your character possesses are shown to the reader in the words on the page.

- Exercise 1: The Great Character. In this exercise, you remind yourself of the reader's experience of a character. You also make sure the character you've created in your mind is making it to the page.

Chapter 3

Going from Blank to Real with Character Traits

WHO'S A BLANK SLATE?

The Victorians, with their scientific revolutions and desire to shape society based on ideals of human perfection, popularized John Locke's notion that a newborn baby is a *tabula rasa*, a blank slate. That means every baby can become exactly what you want it to become, provided you supply it with the proper experiences and education. The Victorian notion of innocence and the empty mind comes down fully on the side of nurture in the *nature-nurture* debate. The Victorians may have brought home indoor plumbing and electricity, but their ideals popularized a fear of spoiling children with affection and the cultural penchant for white bread.

Writers may be the only people who
truly get to work with the blank slate.
When it comes to characters, you are
beginning with a tabula rasa and get to
build an entire person. These characters
will become anything you want them
to become, because you decide their
nature and their nurture in full.

It takes time to discover who a character really is, and there's no point in going about it willy-nilly. There is nothing random about your character. You choose the sex and whether he has his mother's eyes. You decide if he's got an addictive personality or learning disability. You also define his past, his politics, his faith, his profession, how much he wants to change the world, and even what he'll wear when he steps out into that world.

TIME AND INK

Start with the big picture. Before you begin developing your character, you need to know what kind of character he is: star, extra, or something in between? How much time and attention you put into developing each character will depend on how big a part he has in the story. We can think of our characters stacked on a pyramid. The higher up the stack, the better developed a character needs to be. Let's borrow some terms from theatre and film.

POV Character

Primary Characters

Secondary Characters

Tertiary Characters

Your *point of view* (POV)/main character is the lead role. She is at the pinnacle of the pyramid and requires the most development, because she is the reader's means of experiencing your story. Focus your efforts on this character. If you have multiple point of view characters, they all need equal attention. If you think your point of view characters are not all worthy of the top of the pyramid, then axe or demote the characters you don't see as equal. To have a point of view is a special gift, and it has to be earned. Your point of view character must be fully realized. Know her the way you know your spouse or best friend of twenty years. You know her history, her family, her secrets, her problems, her cravings, her pet peeves, what makes her laugh, her bad habits. . . .

Primary characters are in supporting roles. These are important characters, which is why there's a category for them at the Oscars®. These characters need to be fully realized the way you know your good friends and family. These characters are critical to the story and interact with the point of view character the most. They have personalities and depth. Readers might even like them better than the point of view character, even though the *primary characters* are not as deeply involved in the plot.

Make sure your primary characters don't get more than their fair share of the spotlight. It's fine to steal the scene, but not the show. If your main character relies on her best friend to save her, she's no longer the hero. The point of view character must get herself into and out of trouble. Your primary character might save your hero's life, but it has to be the exception, not the rule. And at the end of the story, it has to be the hero who saves the day and is a different person as a result.

In *Dark Corners in Skoghall*, I need my point of view character, Jess, to enter the climactic scene with the villain by herself. She has this very concerned boyfriend, Beckett, who would never let her walk into a trap without him by her side. And no reasonable person would want to, so of course Jess and Beckett would pursue the villain together. This creates a problem. I need Jess to be the hero, to finish her conflict with the villain herself, without relying on help from her boyfriend or anyone else. So I send Beckett to Duluth. He has to go far enough away from Skoghall that he can't reach her in time to thwart the villain—and the climax of my story! To make sure this doesn't seem too convenient or coincidental, I establish early in the book that Beckett has an art show coming up at a gallery in Duluth and mention it more than once as he prepares new pottery for the show.

Your point of view character must be at the center of your plot, have agency, and fulfill her character arc. Self-reliance and determinism are major components of being a hero. That's why in so many hero stories the mythos clearly states, "There can be only one."

Note: There are exceptions to every rule, like when you are writing about a family or collective of superheroes. Also note, however, that the rules of craft can be shaped to accommodate those exceptions.

Secondary characters are in minor supporting roles as recurring characters. They're the familiar faces we enjoy seeing around town. They have names and *dialogue*, spoken lines, but they aren't critical to the plot and aren't major players in the point of view character's life. Some are more familiar and more important than others, but they remain in the middle layer of the pyramid. These characters are disposable. We might miss them, but we probably won't mourn them. Not for long, anyway.

Secondary characters, because they are both familiar and disposable, constitute a good stable of characters for the writer of a series. When you need someone to do something, you simply pick the most likely candidate from your stable and put him to work. For example, in the first Skoghall Mystery book, we meet a teenager who is a rather unlikable waiter at the café. He adds a bit of color to the scene, but that's all. He appears again in the second book, just as briefly. In a future book, he will get mixed up in a murder and possibly die. For readers of the series, it will be fun to see the evolution of the character, yet I doubt anyone will miss him once he's gone.

Tertiary characters are extras and walk-ons. They typically don't have a name and if they have dialogue, it's brief and unremarkable. In movie credits, the character is identified by what he did, not who he is: truck driver, soldier, waiter, or boy with dog.

Don't waste ink on these *tertiary characters*. Give them enough shape and color to keep the read interesting, but don't name them, and don't go into extensive detail about them. Doing so would slow the action of your scene by shifting the reader's focus away from what matters to something he is allowed to forget as soon as the point of view character moves on.

POV: Jess

Primary: Beckett, Tyler, Shakti, Isabella

Secondary: Dave, Lora, Marlene, Sterling, Mike, Carrie, Miss Grundi

Tertiary: Librarian, Waitress, Old Man with Shed

Note: We'll discuss developing the point of view character, but remember that the same methods apply to any character. The lower on the pyramid, the fewer methods and less detail you need to develop the character.

WHAT BEFORE WHO: YOUR CHARACTER'S ROLE IN YOUR STORY

Before you develop *who* your character is, you need to know *what* your character is. In other words, you have to step back from the character and take a look at the story. Developing your point of view character and developing your story go hand in hand. Your main character, no matter who she is, will have to fulfill a certain *role* to be the key player in your plot. You have to create a character who is able to fulfill that role.

For example, if I am going to write a crime thriller, my main character will probably be a police officer or FBI agent. Maybe a private detective. If my character is an at-home mom, I have to ask myself how she is going to come up with the skills required to survive the plot events of a crime thriller. It is possible to have a mom as protagonist in a crime thriller. Doing so, however, means your plot will involve things like babysitters and carpooling. It also means your mom might have to give up the chase to get home before the school bus. This kind of unlikely hero can go in either of two directions: light or dark.

The unlikely hero, a mom in our example, can be found in lighter stories, like romantic comedies. In lighter stories there is more room for humor and the character's mistakes probably won't be fatal. In a darker story, our mom hero will risk orphaning her children when she confronts the bad guys. That is something you, as the writer, have to keep in mind when you develop your character, which is why you need to know what your character is before you develop who your character is. If our hero is a "soccer mom" at the open of the story, part of her journey will be developing the skills she needs to both survive and protect her family. If she used to be a spy who retired to live a family life, then she already has the skills she needs to survive; she just has to dust them off and get back to work.

> At this stage, you only need a basic understanding of your plot in order to develop your character. The premise is enough.

For *The Murder in Skoghall,* my premise is that a woman buys a haunted house and solves a forty-year-old murder mystery to save her home.

Jess, my main character, buys an old farmhouse, only to discover a murdered woman haunts it. Leaving the house would certainly be the simplest course of action, but if Jess ran, I wouldn't have a story. So I had to create the kind of person who would stay and fight for her house. Not only that, she couldn't be the type of person to hold an exorcism and move on; no, she has to put the ghost to rest. Knowing the premise of my book made apparent some of the *traits,* distinguishing characteristics, I would have to assign my character as I developed her, like courage and tenacity.

> Defining what your character is, her role in the plot, will help you shape who your character needs to be in order to fulfill that role.

Here are some basic questions you can answer about your character's role in your story that will help you begin shaping this person.

1. What does your character need to do?

Over the course of the story, your character will need to do a variety of things to survive your plot. These things will require certain qualities and skills. *Qualities* are those things inherent in your character, like personality traits. *Skills* are those things that are learned. Skills may have been acquired before the story began, or they can be learned along the way to the *climax*, the culminating event in which the main conflict reaches its zenith.

If your character needs to defuse a bomb in the climax, he will need the quality *calm under pressure*. He is also going to need the skill *knowledge about bombs*. If he has to perform surgery . . . you get the idea.

Let's look at Jess again. She needs a certain set of qualities, like stubbornness, fearlessness, commitment, and empathy. She's going to need a variety of skills, like interviewing witnesses, conducting research, communicating with spirits, and surviving attacks. At the beginning of *The Murder in Skoghall,* Jess has only some of the skills she needs to survive the haunting. She does, however, have the inherent qualities, and she develops the skills as she goes. In the skills category, your character might need to learn karate or statistical analysis. These are specific skills you can show on the page, so when it's time for your character to use them, the reader believes your character is capable.

Jess has to learn to communicate with a ghost. Initially, this is something that scares her, but as she works with the new ability, it becomes a valuable skill. In *Dark Corners in Skoghall,* Jess learns to fire a gun. It's a skill she puts to use in the book's climax.

Every hero, no matter the type of story, must acquire certain skills as part of his journey. In *The Hero with a Thousand Faces,* Joseph Campbell discusses "the hero's journey." The journey typically begins with an unaware and unlikely hero. The hero doesn't have the skills he needs, but he has the qualities, often unbeknownst to him. Luke Skywalker doesn't know becoming a Jedi is his birthright. Harry Potter doesn't know he's fated to become a powerful wizard. Buffy the Vampire Slayer doesn't know how or why she is the chosen one. Jess doesn't know she can communicate with ghosts. They have the qualities inherent by virtue of birthright or fate, but the knowledge and skills required by the plot have to be learned. Note that becoming self-aware, developing new skills, and becoming self-sufficient over a series of trials compose most of the hero's character arc, that is the hero's evolution over the course of the story. Only then can he save the rest of us.

2. What life lessons does your character need to learn?

At the end of your story, your character will be a different person than at the beginning of your story by virtue of what he has learned. He will need to learn both skills, which we've discussed in the previous section, and also life lessons.

While skills are tangible things that can be taught, like tying your shoes or magical dueling, *life lessons* are intangible and are gained through experience. In fiction, that experience *is* the story. Whatever you decide to put your protagonist through between the front cover and the back cover will result in his personal growth. Your character might need to learn how to let someone love him. Or how to accept help. Or how to be alone in the world.

Jess is learning about inner strength and resilience. Because I'm writing a series, Jess won't have one massive epiphany and become a better person. She will learn something in each book that helps her evolve over the series into a self-reliant, tough, skilled medium-detective.

3. Where does your character live and work?

When deciding your character's traits, you need to factor in setting. Setting is the where and when of your story. A woman of 1868 will have a different set of traits than a woman of 1968 than a woman of 2068. Likewise, if your story is set on a spaceship, your character will need a different set of traits than if your story is set in the Wild West.

Of course, a military spaceship and a military submarine might not be that different. But we need only compare the U.S.S. *Enterprise* and the TARDIS to see that not all spaceships are created equal. You need to be specific about your where and when in order to shape your character.

Jess is a native of Minneapolis, a large urban center in America's Midwest. As such, she has a different set of ideas about the world and her role in it than if she'd come from New York City or a ranch in Wyoming or the Hollywood Hills of Los Angeles. She moves to Skoghall, Wisconsin, a small arts community on the Mississippi River. Part of my character's journey is adapting to a new environment and a new set of people who don't necessarily share her values.

4. What genre are you writing?

The final and broadest question we'll ask ourselves is what genre of story this will be. Each *genre*, or category of fiction, such as science fiction, literary, fantasy, romance, etc., comes with reader expectations. If you're writing an adventure story, a handsome rogue is more likely to be well received than an overweight, balding guy. If you develop an overweight, balding action hero, you may be writing a satire or a comeback story. If your goal is to create an unconventional action hero, be careful. Disappointing reader expectations can easily upset readers. If done well, however, defying reader expectations can delight readers.

There are two approaches you can take to genre and reader expectations. Either write what you want to and then decide which genre it fits into, or study the genres and make sure you include widely accepted traits in your point of view character. Either approach can work, but if you are writing within a genre from the get-go, you'll be wise to understand genre conventions before you start building your character.

Choose your character's traits to either fulfill reader expectations or to surprise and delight readers in lieu of being conventional.

EXERCISE 2: FOUR BASIC QUESTIONS THAT SHAPE CHARACTER

Answer the four basic questions for your character.

Note: All of the exercises in this book can be applied to any character you've already created to help you further develop him. At this point, however, I recommend you grab that *tabula rasa* and begin anew. It will be enlightening to build a character from scratch as you work through this book.

1. Begin with a sentence or two about your scenario. If you aren't sure how to write your scenario, ask yourself what you want to write about. Do you want to write a ghost story? That was the decision that launched Skoghall. I needed a place where a ghost and a person could interact, and a haunted house was as good as any. I needed a protagonist to survive the haunting, and I picked a newly divorced woman who just relocated to a small town.

2. Now that you have your scenario, go ahead and answer those four basic questions about your character's role in your story. Here are the questions again.
    -   What does your character need to do?
        Define the skills and qualities your character will need over the course of the story.
    -   What life lessons does your character need to learn?

Define the intangible skills your character will need to pick up over the course of the story. Also examine the life lessons your character needs to tackle.

- Where does your character live and work?
Define the setting your character inhabits and how that will affect who he is.

- What genre are you writing?
Consider your readers' expectations and whether you'll meet those expectations or surprise and delight your readers with an unconventional protagonist.

GETTING TO KNOW YOUR CHARACTER

Now that you've answered these questions, you have a good sense of the skills and qualities your character needs to fill the role your scenario, setting, and genre demand. Still, that's only a sketch of a person. In the rest of this chapter, I'll explain how to build your character from the tabula rasa up.

In the theatre and the movies, there are actors, costume designers, makeup artists, hairdressers, and props masters who all influence the presentation of character. In literature, you, the writer, need to be an all-in-one creative force. You might begin with the *tabula rasa*, but by the time you finish with your character, you need to have a full-color, three-dimensional, ready-to-jump-off-the-page person. It's easier to start on the outside and work your way into the center.

This approach is not unlike getting to know a real person. You first get a sense of appearance and general traits, then you learn his personality, some of his inherent qualities, his past, his strengths and weakness, likes and dislikes, flaws, and everything else that makes him unique.

Let's take that sketch of a person and send him to wardrobe, makeup, and so on. Then we'll put him on our psychiatrist's couch and go deep into his psyche, until he's finally ready to enter the stage of the page and make that brilliant first impression on your reader!

THE SURFACE

1. Begin with a Body

You probably have a picture of your character in your head. If you don't see pictures in your mind's eye in high definition, you might have found pictures of a model or actor you think your character looks like. That's great, but the reader won't have either of those pictures before her when she reads your book. You're going to have to put that image into words.

Start by writing a description of your character. Describe your character's facial features, her hair, her smile. What's her body type? A triathlete will look different than a tired mother of three. What makes her self-conscious? The prosthetic arm? The mole on her neck? Everyone is self-conscious about something, large or small. And her degree of feeling doesn't have to be proportionate to the issue—the person with the mole could have a tougher time coping than the person with the prosthetic. Remark on anything distinguishable about her physical appearance.

2. Send Him to Wardrobe

Don't put your character in jeans and a T-shirt; it's too generic. Think about your setting. If the book opens in Minneapolis, Minnesota, in January, your reader will meet your character in winter in a cold climate in an urban setting. Say we're meeting her in a café. She'll need a coat, some boots, mittens, and a hat. After she drapes her outerwear over her chair, making sure her coat's not touching the floor, which has dirty slush on it, check out her outfit. She's in Minneapolis, so she'll be metropolitan. How old is she? She might be showing off tattoos, which could require a more open neckline or short sleeves. It's January, so either she is really committed to showing her ink, or she's stripped off a few layers—coat, scarf, sweater. She might have a piercing or dreadlocks. She might be getting a chai after her yoga class, in which case she'll be wearing yoga pants and layers she can shed as she warms up. She might be a student in a hoodie, leggings, and Ugg boots.

See how much we can learn about a character from the first glimpse? That is what you need to provide a reader when you introduce a character, that first impression of a person.

3. Put Her in the Makeup Chair

After you decide your character's physical appearance and wardrobe, move her into makeup. Pay attention to detail. Does she have a messy bun or a carefully coifed do? Is she scrubbed clean or wearing kohl eyeliner? And if he's a man? How about tattoos? Facial hair? Earrings? Hairstyle? Anything to do with grooming is part of your character's presentation on the page, just like it's part of your presentation to the world whenever you step outside your door.

4. Give Her Some Props

People like stuff, and characters are no different. *Props* is short for properties, and it's all the stuff your character handles over the course of the story, as well as objects that decorate your character's environment. As you get to know your character, consider not only what is worn or carried, but how it is worn or carried and its condition.

Take a closer look at your character. Holes in jeans could be a sign of poverty, slovenliness, or style. She might carry a chemistry textbook, but is she the professor or the student? An antique pocket watch, a Fitbit, and a Rolex send different messages about the wearer. A military crew cut is worn by a different person than a topknot and soul patch. A Timbuk2 messenger bag accessorizes a different life than a Prada tote.

EXERCISE 3: THE POWER OF OBSERVATION

In this exercise, we'll discover how much significant information is available in a visual impression of a person and how to make that work for you and your character.

Part One:

1. Next time you're in a café, do some people watching. Notice someone in detail, and make a list of everything you can determine about that person. It doesn't matter if you're right or wrong—unless you show him the list! You'll see you

don't just get a description of physical appearance, but a sense of this person's lifestyle and values.

2. Now that you have an exhaustive list of visible traits, set a timer for fifteen minutes and freewrite. The rules of freewriting are simple: Get out paper and pencil. Set a timer. Start writing. Don't stop until the timer goes off. Keep your hand moving! If you can't think of anything to write, write "I don't know what to write," over and over, until something new comes to you.

3. Write about a character with those traits you just wrote down. Give him a voice and something to do. Give him someone to interact with. Set your timer for fifteen minutes. Ready. Set. Go!

Part Two:

1. Imagine your new character, the one you're developing, walking into the café to meet somebody for coffee. Watch her. Go ahead and really stare. Make a list of all her visible traits and all the things you can surmise about her and her lifestyle based on her appearance.

   You now have a list of visible traits you can use throughout your story to signify who your character is to other characters and *your readers*.

2. Write a scene with your character based on that list of traits. What kind of stuff does she carry? What drink does she order at the counter? What about her body language? Use

her appearance as the basis of the entire scene, like you did in part one of this exercise.

Now you better understand how to use your character's physical appearance, movement, mannerisms, and handling of objects when you show her acting *in scene,* carrying out physical movements that could be tracked visually on the stage of the page. This is a critical part of storytelling. As you learned in Exercise 1, if it's not on the page, it's not being communicated to the reader.

UNDER THE SURFACE

You've already discovered a lot about your character by identifying what he needs to do and learn, where and when he lives, and by creating a physical picture of him. But we are more than our physical composite. From somewhere within, we develop an array of character traits that combine to make us like some, different from others, and unique. That last bit is important: *unique.*

Grab your snorkel. Time to go beneath the surface.

When you create a point of view character, you need to strive for a special combination of traits that will create the heart of your story. As you develop your character, you will need to know your character's history, even if ninety-five percent of it never makes it onto the page. You are setting out to create a three-dimensional, living, breathing, autonomous being. When you create a real-life character, your readers will treat him like a real-life person. That kind of engagement is what turns readers into fans.

If you want to create a character with the potential to be iconic, the kind of character people tell their friends about, remember long after they've forgotten your name, then forget the snorkel. Grab your scuba gear!

THE CASE FOR SPECIFICITY

You might be tempted to think that a less specific character would be easier to relate to, because the reader could superimpose himself over your character; however, the opposite is true. Lack of specificity is the kiss of death for characters. We relate to real people, not types.

Everyone likes an everyman character, so long as he's different from every man.

If your character is generic, it's because you haven't drilled down deep enough into her history and psyche. Such a character can seem bland to a reader. Such a character should never reach a reader's hands. Fortunately, bland characters have a built-in safety switch: they're difficult to write. You'll get Ms. Flat into a sticky situation, then find yourself uncertain how she should react. You don't really know if that line of dialogue sounds natural coming out of her mouth. Dull characters sound so similar to each other that, if you didn't have dialogue tags, a reader wouldn't know who's saying what. And if you put a generic character in a crowded room, she'd be hard to pick out from everyone else. Not exactly the stuff of a memorable story, so let's get deep and specific about that character you're developing.

Joe is a male, American, middle-class, college-educated, white-collar office worker, earning around $60,000, living in Minneapolis, childless, who likes to sail in summer and ski in winter.

All of that makes Joe pretty special. You can write a story about Joe now.

But wait.

Phil is a male, American, middle-class, college-educated, white-collar office worker, earning around $60,000, living in Minneapolis, childless, who likes to sail in summer and ski in winter.

All of that makes Phil pretty special. You can write a story about Phil now.

Except, in reality, neither Joe nor Phil are special. Not yet, anyway.

The more you know about your characters' lives …

Joe grew up
in rural Minnesota.

Phil grew up
in Chicago.

… on and off the page …

Joe was raised
Catholic.

Phil was
raised Jewish.

... before, during and after the story ...

Joe has been married 15 years.

Phil got divorced 5 years ago.

This is Joe

This is Phil

... the richer your characters will be ...

Joe lost a child.

Phil never had any.

This is Joe

This is Phil

... the better you will understand them ...

Phil's mother
has Alzheimers.

Joe's parents are healthy.

... and the more your readers will care about them.

Phil does improv
on the weekends.

Joe has a stutter.

Joe has a cataract.

Phil is missing a finger.

Now you can begin to write about Joe and Phil.

The more the dots diverge, the more interesting your characters become. Even if every trait listed for Joe and Phil is history that never makes it onto the page, it's still meaningful. Your life experiences shape how you interact with the here and now, and the same is true for your characters. Joe carries an emotional scar for the child he lost. Phil has recently dealt with elder care. Those experiences will affect how the characters interact with circumstances and people in their lives throughout the story.

You need to know your character intimately, and through your story, your reader should get to know your character intimately. Let's start building that memorable, engaging, unique character.

EXERCISE 4: CHARACTER BUILDING WORKSHEET

This list of questions will help you understand your character from the surface to the deep history. Your answers to these questions will show you how your character will interact with the world, especially when combined with the questions you've already answered about your character's role. That means knowing how your character thinks, feels, acts, and reacts throughout your story.

Grab your journal and write out each question, and answer it in as much detail as you can before writing down the next question. As you go, expect ideas to come to you regarding how a trait or piece of history could play out. If you write "Education: Seminary," it might next occur that your character could quote scripture as one of his quirky traits. That might not always be welcome by the other characters in the scene, which could make for some nice tension on the page. By answering these questions and expanding to include the ideas that spin off of each answer, you'll soon discover a living being on the page.

1. Full name:
   - Goes by:
2. Demographics
   - Age:
   - Sex/Gender/Orientation:
   - Marital status:
   - Religion:
   - Race or cultural heritage:
   - Nationality:

      –   Childhood home (location):

      –   Currently resides (location):

      –   Political leaning:

3.   Physical Description:

4.   Education:

5.   Profession:

6.   Family structure, including pets:

7.   Habits (good and bad):

8.   Pastimes/Hobbies:

9.   How would his/her best friend describe him/her?

10.   How would an ex-friend or ex-lover describe him/her right after the breakup?

11.   Health condition in general and specifically:

12.   Long- or short-term disabilities or frailties:

13.   What does he/she most like about him/herself?

14.   What does he/she most dislike about him/herself?

15.   What did he/she want to be when he/she grew up?

16.   How did accomplishing that or not accomplishing that affect his/her outlook on life?

17.   Is he/she a Type A or Type B personality?

18.   In what areas of life would he/she call him/herself a success? A failure?

19.   How does he/she feel about romance? About sex?

20.   How would he/she describe his/her most important relationship (spouse, parent, child, friend)?

21.   What is his/her great disappointment in life?

22.   What is his/her pet peeve?

23.   What is his/her greatest weakness?

24. What does he/she hold dearest in this world?

25. What does he/she fear?

26. How does this feared thing manifest in his/her life?

27. What does he/she want more than anything else?

28. Why does he/she want that?

29. How would he/she be changed by getting it?

30. How would he/she be changed by *not* getting it?

RECAP

In this chapter, we've begun building a character from the outside in. We began with the type of story you're writing, moved on to your character's role, then to his appearance, and then went deep into his psyche. The basis for getting to know your character is a process of questions and answers. As you work through this process, you'll find ideas start flowing to build your story around its heart, your point of view character.

- Writers are probably the only people who get to work with a *tabula rasa*. Lucky us!

- Know what kind of character you're writing: point of view, primary, secondary, or tertiary. The higher up the pyramid, the more effort you'll need to put into character development.

- Your story's plot will make demands on your character's development by dictating many of the things he needs to do and learn to carry your reader through the story. Have a rudimentary understanding of your plot before you develop your character. Knowing your premise is enough to begin with.

- Know what your main character needs to know and do over the course of the story. Consider both her qualities and her skills.
- Know what your character has to learn and how he will change over the course of the story.
- Your setting will help you shape your character. Your character may love or hate that place she calls home, but that place comes with other people and their belief systems, lifestyle, amenities, traffic, and many other factors that impact how she gets through her day.
- Exercise 2: Four Basic Questions that Shape Character. You discover the demands your story makes on your character.
- Start with your character's surface traits, like appearance, and work your way deep into his psyche. Make sure the traits you assign your character are specific enough to build a unique person.
- Exercise 3: The Power of Observation. You understand how much we learn about people and characters from appearance alone, and how important those visual cues are in character development.
- To build believable characters readers will empathize with, you need to know your character intimately.
- Give your character a unique combination of trails and experiences to make her worth writing.

- Exercise 4: Character Building Worksheet. After answering these thirty questions about your character, you'll probably know her as well as you know anybody. Writing out your answers to these questions should generate ideas about how traits might manifest within your story, contributing to meaningful moments on the page.

Chapter 4

Nobody's Perfect

FLAWS, FATAL FLAWS, AND PLOT

Fiction is bad things happening to interesting people. I think I got this from my high school English teacher, Roger Mahn. I like how concise it is. That sentence reduces all of fiction down to two simple premises: first, shit happens; second, your character can't be boring. And anyone without a flaw is boring.

Remember the *tabula rasa*? The perfect baby who has yet to be subjected to the vagaries of life? What kind of story could you write about such a character? No kind, because the character would not be interesting. The exception to that rule is, naturally, Mary Poppins, but even she is only *"practically* perfect in every way."

"Aha!" you say. Mary Poppins is outrageously popular. Beloved by generations. I just admitted she's perfect, practically perfect at least. Doesn't old Mary Poppins prove me wrong?

No.

Mary Poppins is an exception to the rule and one worth a mention. Mary Poppins, the title character of P.L. Travers's *Mary Poppins,* is an example of a special kind of fantasy. In this type of fantasy, the protagonist is remarkably charming and fascinating, which facilitates readers' love of her. Readers, however, do not empathize with Mary Poppins. They empathize with the Banks, the frazzled family in need of rescue. Readers long for a real-life Mary Poppins to blow onto their front stoop, slide up their banister, and fix their lives. In fact, although Mary Poppins is the hero of the tale, it's not her story. She is a vehicle through which the Banks's story is told. Mary Poppins is wonderful, but she is too perfect and too without conflict to be relatable. We do not identify with Mary Poppins. *We want her help.* The Banks family, on the other hand, we can understand and get behind them, and when Mary Poppins leaves them flying a kite, we even envy them a little.

Mary Poppins aside, if nobody's perfect, then your character shouldn't be either. Having a rough edge or two can make your character more likable and sympathetic to your readers. In fact, we often find characters more sympathetic precisely *because* they are struggling with a flaw.

Flaws are anything your character is or does that is less than ideal that affects the plot. They can be temporary or permanent. They can come from a twist of fate or poor choices. They can be physical or emotional. Wherever they originate and whatever their form, they are things the hero must overcome.

The *fatal flaw* forms the crux of the character arc. It is so deep seated the character usually isn't even aware of it. Yet your character's fatal flaw will be his downfall if he does not resolve it. To do so, your character must have an epiphany and change, so he is a different person at the end of the story than at the beginning, bringing the character arc to fruition.

To understand the role of a character's flaws better, let's look at the fairy tale, "Beauty and the Beast."

CURSED CURSES!

Fairy tales use symbolism without subtlety, which makes them handy for a quick analysis. In the first published adaptation of "Beauty and the Beast," the tale is allegorical. Jeanne-Marie Leprince de Beaumont's adaptation, originally published in *Magasin des Enfants* in 1756, was used to teach girls the rewards of virtue and to prize kindness in their suitors over good looks and wit. We have a beautiful maiden and a hideous beast. The beast is really a handsome prince who has been cursed to look like a beast. He is named for his outward, physical flaw. But that is not his fatal flaw. The concern of the plot is that he must break the curse before time runs out, or he'll be ugly forever. The fatal flaw, which is internal and the crux of his character arc, is that the young prince is stingy and selfish. He refused shelter to an old woman, who happened to be a fairy, and she cursed him.

Beast has limited time to break the curse. In some versions, including Disney's, he is angry about his fate, another flaw, and must control his anger to avoid scaring Beauty while showing her as much generosity as possible. However, his generosity must be sincere, not simply a showering of gifts, but meaningful sacrifices for Beauty's happiness. Beauty must see beyond his appearance and fall in love with him despite his beastliness. True gentleness, generosity, and love cannot be faked. When the Beast overcomes his fatal flaw, thus winning Beauty's love, the curse is broken and they live happily ever after.

In that fairy tale, we can easily see how the character's flaws create obstacles and make the desired outcome less assured. If Beast cannot control his anger, Beauty will be too frightened of him to see beyond his appearance. If Beast cannot discover true generosity in his own heart, he will not be worthy of Beauty's love, and the curse will become permanent.

> Your character's flaws become his
> own personal, portable obstacles to
> overcome on the path to his goal.

SO MANY FLAWS, SO LITTLE TIME

You can choose your character's flaws the same way you choose her good traits. It's important to choose these flaws consciously so that they matter to the character, the plot, and the reader.

If your character is a clumsy oaf, and his oafishness is charming, it's not a flaw. It's a trait. If your character is a clumsy oaf trying desperately to impress a beautiful girl, it becomes a flaw, because his oafishness impacts his self-esteem, the way the girl sees him, and because the reader will recognize it as a complication between him and his goal—getting the girl.

> # A flaw will create a complication between your character and his goal.

Let's revisit the four basic questions that shape character (from chapter three). Only this time, we'll use them as a means to discover our character's flaws, so think about her negative side.

1. What does your character need to do?

Over the course of the story, your character will need to do a variety of things to survive your plot based on your character's role in the story. Given your character's role, does it make sense for her to be a workaholic? Or trapped in an unhappy relationship? Or to feel underappreciated? Or to have a substance abuse problem? Or to self-harm? A criminal attorney might be a workaholic. An addict might be a liar. A celebrity might use her friends.

Let's look at some possible scenarios and related character flaws. We'll base our exploration on questions and scenarios already posed in chapter three.

Scenario: If your character needs to defuse a bomb in the climax, he will need the quality *calm under pressure*. He is also going to need the skill *knowledge about bombs*. If he has to perform surgery...you get the idea.

Flaws: Ask, what flaw would complicate being responsible for defusing a bomb? I can think of a few.

- He has a tremor from nerve damage, PTSD-related stress, or detoxing from an addiction. Your character is going to have a harder time cutting the right wire if his hand is shaking as time is running out.
- He has an active addiction. His friend gets him to the scene in time to help, but he's not exactly sober.
- His mother was killed in an explosion and his greatest fear is dying by explosion. He freezes up when faced with the bomb.

A good trait, like tenacity, can become a flaw, like stubbornness. Jess saves her house because she refuses to give it up. Had I desired a different outcome, I could have put her in denial and made it so she didn't recognize when to give up. I have no plans to kill Jess, but I've already hurt her quite a bit, and her tenacity, I mean stubbornness, is behind much of it. In fact, that very trait is both a good quality and a flaw in Jess. She saved her house, because she wouldn't let it go. But she almost lost Beckett, because she wouldn't let Tyler go.

2. What life lessons does your character need to learn?

At the end of your story, your character will be a different person than at the beginning of your story by virtue of what he has learned.

Scenario: Your character might need to learn how to let someone love him. Or how to accept help. Or how to be alone in the world.

Flaws: Suppose he needs to learn to let someone love him. Then an obvious flaw is that he has constructed emotional barriers. He won't let his guard down and trust anyone. These are flaws, because, while they might once have been a defense mechanism, now they stand in the way of his happiness.

If he needs to learn how to accept help, his flaw could be that he does everything himself. This probably drives people away, and he'll find himself alone when he most needs help. That will create a major complication in any story.

Jess is learning about inner strength and resilience. She's tortured in *Dark Corners in Skoghall*. In the next book, *Don't Get Stuck in Skoghall,* Jess will suffer some serious repercussions before finding the resources within to get back on her feet.

3. Where does your character live and work?

When deciding your character's traits, you need to factor setting into the kind of person he is, the kind of skills he has, and the kind of experiences he faces. Setting is the where and when of your story.

Scenario: If you're writing about a Victorian woman, she could face authority figures in her mother, her husband, her pastor, and her boss if she is a servant or factory worker.

Flaws: She might reject authority, which gets her into trouble with some or all of those people in her life.

Jess moves to a rural community from a city. One of her flaws might be that she moves a trunk full of stereotypes. These suppositions could get in the way of her making friends when she needs them. She might develop foot-in-mouth disease or rub everyone the wrong way. She doesn't, but I do have fun writing minor characters who defy and confirm stereotypes, just like real people.

4. What genre are you writing?

Each genre comes with reader expectations. If you're writing an adventure story with a handsome rogue for your protagonist, readers might expect him to be a bit of a womanizer.

Scenario: It is normal to find a hardened police detective with a drinking problem. Readers might even expect it, because the work is known to be demanding, stressful, and ugly. Likewise, readers will expect a twelve-year-old girl to gossip about her best friend's crush.

Flaws: If you reverse the problems, creating a hardened detective who gossips about his coworkers and a twelve-year-old alcoholic, you've either got a problem or you're on your way to writing a fresh take on the flawed character. Maybe the detective is teased by his colleagues for staying on top of everyone else's business, but that tendency to gossip turns into something more sinister, like blackmail. Sometimes kids start young.

There is nothing wrong with working *with* reader expectations. Detectives and drink? It goes with the job, after all. Subverting types and expectations can be incredibly powerful, but it has to work for the story. If your detective is a gossip, you'd better use it at some point, even if only in a lighthearted way. If your little girl is tipping a bottle, that is probably the focus of your story. Subverting reader expectations can be the best way to keep things fresh.

Choose your character's flaws to either fulfill reader expectations or to surprise and delight readers in lieu of being conventional.

THE POOR, MESSED-UP, LIKABLE, SYMPATHETIC CHARACTER

Whatever your story's parameters, remember to balance redeeming qualities with flaws. Stories about really messed-up people—the addict who gets clean, the orphan who finds family, the sinner who forgives himself—tend to be stories of triumph over struggle. Why? Because really messed-up people aren't that much fun to be around. Like our characters, readers need to have something to desire for a character they *sympathize* with. If the sinner desires forgiveness, we can get behind that. If the orphan is resourceful, resilient, and fun to hang with (think Anne, Annie, and Harry), we're willing to explore the dark side of being an orphan in order to get to the other side, the side where the orphan gets the family.

If your character's flaw is too big or unrelatable, and it's *not* balanced with redeeming qualities, you'll risk losing readers who don't want to go on that ride. Imagine the vivacious orphan going to school and bullying younger kids. It would ruin several classics. Even if we understood the motivation behind it—after all, none of those orphans were treated well before their lucky breaks—we could not condone the flawed behavior. The character would seem undeserving of a triumphant climax. In storyspeak, the protagonist has to be *likable* enough to seem deserving of any good fortune that comes his way. And likable enough to seem a tragic figure when misfortune comes his way.

Make sure you balance your
character's flaws with her redeeming
qualities, or you risk losing readers
who find her unsympathetic.

ISN'T A FATAL FLAW JUST A REALLY BIG FLAW?

A flaw is anything your character is or does that is less than ideal *and* that affects the plot arc. Nail biting probably won't ruin or save the day, so it's a negative trait, a bad habit. Drinking to excess could incapacitate the hero when he's needed, so it's a flaw.

If the hero is incapacitated by drink, isn't that a fatal flaw? No. It's a symptom of the fatal flaw. Why does the hero drink? What is the drink helping him forget or ignore? That is the fatal flaw, the Achilles' heel, the thing that will destroy him if he can't change.

The fatal flaw is the demon inside.
It must be resolved at the end of
the character arc in order for the
character to show real change at
the end of the book or series.

Consider a criminal attorney with one big case after another. Let's call him Steve. One of his flaws is being a workaholic, to the extent that his wife is packing up the kids and leaving him. Being a workaholic is a flaw that is a symptom of the fatal flaw. Only resolving the fatal flaw will win back his family. What is the fatal flaw? Hubris. Steve believes it is up to him and him alone to put away the bad guy. This belief gets in the way of him supporting the people he loves. If he can't change that hubristic streak, he'll end up alone, and putting away the bad guy will no longer be as meaningful.

Steve would never blame hubris for his problems. He's fighting the good fight, doing what he has to do to keep his family and society safe. He's convinced his wife is in the wrong. He is a hero, after all, and he has a big old blind spot for his fatal flaw.

Let's continue with our attorney. Steve gets off work at seven o'clock most nights, if he's lucky. He goes from the office to a bar for a glass or two of scotch. It's not that he doesn't want to eat dinner with his family, it's that he's not ready to face them after the things he's seen at work all day. So he unwinds over whisky. Going to the bar and missing time with his family is a flaw, but it's only a symptom of the fatal flaw. Say he goes home, kisses the kids goodnight, and then pours another drink or three, we still haven't gotten to the fatal flaw. His drinking is still only a symptom.

To grow and change, to save his marriage, Steve does not need to go to a recovery program. He does not need to get a new job. He could do both of those things, but only as support systems for correcting his fatal flaw. Of course, Steve could be forced into a recovery program, but the program won't work until he resolves his fatal flaw. That is, if Steve realizes he's been so wrapped up in his self-importance that he's neglected everyone he cares about, his arc will be resolved and he might live happily ever after—or at least more happily than he did on the pages of our book.

The chain of cause and effect is this: Steve *realizes* his hubris has caused him to neglect his loved ones – Steve apologizes to his wife and proves his commitment to change by going into treatment and putting in his notice at work – Steve and his family take a vacation together and the reader ends the book with the belief that he and his family will be happy now.

THE FLAW IN THE PLOT:

Your character's flaw will help shape your plot. This is because your story is your character's journey through a series of events as he resolves his fatal flaw. The plot events are dramatic occurrences that precipitate, facilitate, and illustrate character changes.

A character's flaw cannot be separated from the plot.

In the example of "Beauty and the Beast," we saw that the plot revolves around the character's fatal flaw. In order to break the curse, his goal, Beast must overcome selfishness, his flaw, to win the love of Beauty.

You probably aren't writing an allegorical tale. Your story is probably more complex, with a main plot that is action driven and at least a couple of subplots that are character driven. As such, relating your character's flaws to the plot might seem more complicated than in our fairy tale example. But it needn't be. That's because, at the end of the day, character still drives plot.

Let's look at Steve, our high-powered criminal attorney again. For our plot, Steve needs to bring a dangerous criminal to justice. We've already identified the subplot: Steve's home life is falling apart. We've identified his fatal flaw as hubris. This manifests as several smaller, easily identified flaws, like being a workaholic and drinking to excess. He might also be short-tempered and demanding, given the stress of his job.

Your plot should suggest flaws, and your flaws should suggest plot points. Let's brainstorm a few plot points based on Steve's flaws. He is a short-tempered, self-absorbed workaholic, who drinks too much.

- Because Steve is a workaholic drinker, his wife has kicked him out of the house. The bad guys aren't aware that he's moved to a hotel across from the office, and go to his home to threaten him. Steve isn't there to protect his family.

- Steve's kid gets hurt when the bad guys come to the house. Now Steve is even more driven to bring the criminal to justice, because it's personal. But if he doesn't make time for his family now, his wife will never forgive him. He has to choose between being a father and being a criminal attorney, between being there for his family and getting justice for his family.

- Steve is demanding at work and, in the midst of the biggest case ever, his assistant gets fed up with him and quits, leaving Steve unable to finish the research on the case.

- With everything going on, his drinking worsens and the unthinkable happens. Steve gets sloppy at work. His co-

counsel covers for him, but she's not a friend and now he owes her a big favor.

If we hadn't already identified Steve's flaws, those plot points would make them apparent. As you develop your character, his flaws, and your storyline, brainstorm ways the flaws can affect the plot. If you have trouble coming up with ideas, you may need a different set of flaws, flaws that are more relevant to your plot. If you're satisfied with your flaws, you may need to introduce some new elements into your plot, elements suggested by those flaws.

Note: It is often simplest to discuss story in terms of drama, but the principles apply to comedies and family-friendly stories as well. Take *Anne of Green Gables* by Lucy Maude Montgomery, which is about as humorous and charming as a book can get. One of young Anne Shirley's flaws is that she is passionate and rash. A plot point that bears this out is when Anne breaks her slate over Gilbert Blythe's head. Gilbert is teasing Anne, so although her flaw leads to a rather unkind action, Anne remains sympathetic and likable.

EXERCISE 5: FINDING THE FLAW IN YOUR PLOT

Repeat the brainstorming we just did for Steve, the attorney, using your character. Alternatively, brainstorm some plot points, the story events. As you see what kind of trouble your character can get into, figure out the flaw that makes that trouble possible.

1. Write down your character's fatal flaw. Beneath it, make a list of all the ways this could manifest as smaller, tangible flaws. For example, Steve's hubris leads to him being a workaholic, which leads to him being an alcoholic. If you aren't sure what your character's flaws are, go with what you've got and change them as the plot points suggest better options.

2. Make a list or a mind map of plot points that will raise your character's stakes up to the climax. Don't worry if they're good plot points. Just write down anything and everything. In this process, be outlandish—do not censor yourself.

3. Compare the flaws and the plot points. Would you like to revise the list of flaws or the fatal flaw? Can you strengthen the plot points?

4. Considering what you've identified as your character's fatal flaw and the way it plays out in the plot, what is the *theme* of your book, that is the intangible something that your story is about? For Steve's story, the theme might be the high personal cost of success.

Remember, stories evolve as we write them. This prewriting will help you immensely, but you can always change your mind later. If this exercise is difficult, you might be too nice to your character. Rough him up a bit and get dirty with your plot.

RECAP

In this chapter, we discussed your character's flaws and fatal flaw, how the fatal flaw relates to theme, and how your character's flaws impact your plot.

- A flaw is something negative your character is or does that affects the plot.
- A fatal flaw is the crux of the character arc. Your character must resolve the fatal flaw in order to fulfill a satisfying character arc.
- You choose your character's flaws the same way you choose his positive traits. Examine your character's role in the story, his work, his location, what he needs to do and learn, and your genre.
- Your character's flaws need to be balanced with your character's virtues or he may become unlikable and unsympathetic.
- The fatal flaw is the biggest obstacle to your character's success. Other flaws are simply manifestations of the fatal flaw.
- Your character's flaws will suggest plot points and plot points will suggest flaws. Consider them intricately intertwined.
- Exercise 5: Finding the Flaw in Your Plot. In this exercise, you identify your character's flaws and brainstorm plot points. By examining your lists, you discover the theme of your book.

Chapter 5

The Past Meets the Present: History and Backstory

HISTORY AND BACKSTORY DEFINED

History and backstory are both critical to your story, but for different reasons.

You need to know your character's *history*, or life story, to thoroughly develop that character. History might come to bear on your character's demeanor, accent, social and political beliefs, treatment of animals, attitude toward money, etc. In that sense, history is important to the story you're telling. However, a reader will be able to understand your story without knowing your character's history. History has to do primarily with character motivation. Why does that detective have a passion for helping women who are victims of abuse? The reader may never know that when he was six he saw his father kill his mother.

Your character's *backstory* is critical to the action you're putting on the page, and that's what distinguishes it from history. Backstory consists of parts of the character's past that a reader needs to learn to understand the plot. It differs from history in that it must be included somewhere, somehow on the page so that the reader understands why your character behaves the way he does in the here and now. Why, during questioning, did that detective beat up a man charged with abusing his wife? Because when the detective was six he saw his father kill his mother. And now the detective's lawyer and union rep want to use his childhood trauma to mitigate the charges of police brutality and save his job.

> History drives character development.
> Backstory drives plot.

HISTORY LESSONS

Understanding your point of view character's history is critical to the character development process. Begin by asking yourself more questions about the character. Where did your character grow up? What was the economic situation there? How many adults were in the household? It might have been a single-parent home, or he might have had grandparents or an uncle living with the family. Your character might value family, because he has such fond memories of his childhood, or because it's the thing he lacked as a child. How many siblings did he have? Where did your character go to school? Did he have a religious or a secular upbringing? Was the family affluent or lacking?

Knowing at least some of your primary and secondary characters' histories will help you mold them into dynamic, believable characters.

In *Dark Corners in Skoghall*, Victor Martinez is a primary character. He's the lead investigator on a murder case. His personal history is never on the page, but in developing him as a character who feels real, I created a history for him.

Each year, Victor's parents followed the migrant labor stream out of Mexico, flowing north with the available jobs, from fields to canning factories to turkey farms. Eventually, they were able to settle down in Wisconsin so their children could go to school and have a better, more stable childhood. Victor was born in Wisconsin, after his parents made their permanent home there. With this history, I know Victor is bilingual with strong ties to an immigrant community. Because he works for the sheriff's office, I know he's worked hard to build a career in a profession where racial bias and mistrust create rifts between his colleagues and his home community. He's got to bridge multiple divides every day of his life.

Sometimes a character's history turns up in small ways, but those small ways are important. They can create *verisimilitude*, which is often the difference between a reader believing you "got it right" and believing you "didn't do your homework." For example, I interviewed the Pepin County sheriff while writing *Dark Corners in Skoghall*, because Skoghall is set in a fictional version of Pepin County. The sheriff told me that in a small department, anyone who could speak

Spanish, regardless of rank, would be called to interpret for other officers. As a result, I have a scene in which Victor answers his cell phone and has to go serve as interpreter at a domestic disturbance call. I'm sure most readers won't think anything of that small detail, but for those who know something about law enforcement in small communities, it could be the thing that grants me authority and earns me that reader's trust.

How deep do you need to dive? Deep enough to know your character. How will he react to the events of your story? How will he be affected? How does his history shape his worldview? Go deep, but not so deep it becomes an excuse for never writing the story.

WHO CARES ABOUT BACKSTORY?

Your characters do, and so do your readers. Backstory uses past events that relate to present events to show your readers what makes your characters do what they do. Backstory can consist of happy things, but often it is like picking at a scab: you're exposing a scar or a wound, and it will be deep or fresh or both.

Let's go back to Jess and her ghost problem. If you bought a house and it turned out to be haunted by a violently dangerous ghost, would you stick around or find a new place to live? It might be easier to put the house back on the market and find somewhere else to hang your hat. But not for Jess. She's determined to keep her house. Why? It's not enough to tell the reader Jess won't leave because she's determined. This abstract motivation has to be connected to her life through real events, events that occurred *before* she encountered her ghost. That's where backstory comes in.

Jess is newly divorced. We find out during the early chapters of *The Murder in Skoghall* that Jess's ex refused to leave their house. Instead of peaceably coexisting, he claimed his territory and made Jess feel like an interloper in her own home, destroying her sense of comfort and belonging. Buying the farmhouse with her divorce settlement is a way for her to reclaim her peace, belonging, comfort, and hope for her future. The ghost doesn't only threaten her physical space, but her ideal of home. Thanks to her divorce, Jess is especially motivated to stay in her house.

The reader understands Jess's motivation to stay in the house without being told, because he's been shown the backstory. That example shows us that real events in Jess's past are motivating the choices she makes now. If the divorce was an old wound, if she wasn't so invested in starting over, she might be less tenacious about keeping her new house.

HOW TO CREATE BACKSTORY

When you create backstory, think of the *events* in your character's past that affect the plot of your story. Jess's divorce is a past event that affects how she reacts to her ghost—the haunting is the main plot of the book. There are two simple ways to create backstory. Reverse engineering and forward engineering. Let's do some reverse engineering.

In reverse engineering, start with the plot, the *now*-story. Then work backwards to find or create events in your character's life that you can use in the now.

We'll begin a story about two women, Jill and Marlie. Jill and Marlie met three years ago through a charity event and hit it off. They've been best friends ever since. Our story is about Jill suffering the loss of her unborn baby and the trauma and grief of this often misunderstood type of loss.

Part of the writer's job is to ask, "How can things get worse for my character?" Things can be worse for Jill if her best friend and confidante, Marlie, pulls back and starts avoiding Jill after she loses the baby. Jill doesn't know why Marlie would disappear in her hour of greatest need, and that piles hurt upon hurt.

Right now, we know the plot point: Marlie isn't there for Jill. What we don't know yet is *why* she's not there for Jill or how this can be resolved. We're starting with the problem and working backwards through the character's life to find the backstory that is relevant to this plot point.

Why would Marlie abandon Jill? Think of as many reasons as you can. Pick the biggest, baddest reason, apply it to our story and see how the characters' lives become more complicated, the plot stronger, and the story richer.

Let's say four years ago, before Jill and Marlie met, Marlie suffered a traumatic pregnancy loss that resulted in a hysterectomy. Not only did she have to survive trauma and grieve her lost baby, but she is now sterile. Marlie avoids pregnant women, because her pain is too great. She could barely handle Jill's joy at being pregnant, and now that Jill lost the baby, Marlie has to retreat to save herself.

Marlie's loss is the backstory that comes to bear on the *now*-story, rippling through the plot and increasing our characters' suffering. The backstory can be used to create intrigue. Before we reveal her backstory, Marlie will seem cold and incomprehensible to both Jill and the reader.

The second way to create backstory is to look at your character's history, his life story, and find events in the past that can factor into the now. This is forward engineering.

Let's create a character named Paul. Paul grew up in rural Iowa. When Paul was ten, his father had his arm crushed by a piece of machinery. Paul's father was no longer able to work the farm and they couldn't afford to hire help. Medical bills piled up. The bank refused to give them another loan. Their credit was maxed out. His family lost the farm. His dad collected disability insurance. His mom got an unskilled job at the town library. They left the home Paul's grandfather built to live in a one-bedroom apartment.

That piece of history would certainly shape Paul's feelings about farming, banks, the medical system, and other issues related to his family's fate. All of those attitudes would help determine how Paul acts and reacts in the *now*-story.

Let's say Paul has a nice job in management and he's getting by all right. Then his kid gets sick and the bills pile up. The things that happened to his family when he was a kid will come to bear on the *now*-story. All of the emotion he felt about his parents and the loss of their family home will compound his feelings now. His backstory could motivate him to come back fighting, or it could send him into a tailspin. Either way, that history became backstory when it became relevant to the *now*-story. Your job is to place it on the page for the reader. You can do that in several ways.

> History affects character and may be known by the reader. Backstory affects plot and must be known by the reader.

A NOTE ABOUT REVEALS
AND *THE* REVEAL

Reveal is a wonderful word and it's especially important to writers. In fact, you'll encounter it frequently throughout the rest of this chapter.

My trusty, old *The American Heritage Dictionary*—a Christmas present when I was in high school, missing a corner that my pet rabbit chewed on—tells us that reveal is a transitive verb, meaning "1. To divulge or disclose; make known. 2. To bring to view; show."

Throughout any work of fiction, we must consciously reveal information to the reader. Doing so with careful intention creates a sense of mounting intrigue that builds to the reveal. *Intrigue* consists of the questions writers expect a reader to ask as a result of specific material on the page. *The reveal* is writer's jargon for that moment the established intrigue is resolved and the questions in the reader's mind are answered. Each story will have many reveals, small and large. The later in the story, the bigger the reveal because more ink has been invested in mounting intrigue through the preceding pages of the story.

Here's an example of a series of moments of intrigue (I'm showing the reader things that I expect will lead her to ask specific questions) and reveal (moments that answer the reader's questions established by intriguing clues on the page) that foreshadow trouble to come. In *The Murder in Skoghall,* Tyler often puts his hand on the outside of his jeans pocket. When I show this gesture to the reader, I expect she'll be wondering why he keeps putting his hand on that pocket and what the bulge is. Eventually, I reveal the bulge is a pocketknife. I expect the reader to wonder why he carries that knife around and why he feels the need to touch it so often. The answer is in his backstory. As Jess gets to know him better, the reader eventually learns he's a veteran with PTSD. It is revealed that he carries the pocketknife because of his anxiety, like a deadly security blanket. The potential violence symbolized and foreshadowed by the knife plays out later in the story. Through the crafting of those moments of intrigue and reveal, I have guided my reader through a series of questions to an answer that is unsettling, thereby replacing intrigue with anxiety, which I then deliver on when Tyler attacks Jess.

WHEN AND HOW TO REVEAL BACKSTORY

Backstory should be woven into the story as it becomes relevant to the action. In other words, do not front-load your backstory, trying to explain to the reader who your character is or where she came from. Doing so will slow down your action, causing drag. What's more, it's likely to seem dull, because the reader won't immediately know why he should care. By placing the backstory where it sheds light on the current action, the reader will easily make the connections you need.

> The placement of backstory is
> all about relevance.

There are several ways to effectively reveal backstory: narrative exposition, flashback, and dialogue. Which one you use at any given time depends on the dramatic effect of the backstory on the current action. The greater its effect, the deeper you can go into the *cause* of that effect.

NARRATIVE EXPOSITION

Narrative exposition is writing in your narrator's voice. You can think of it as your authorial voice, if you like. Narrative is the prose that creates mood, sets the scene, paints a picture, reflects, goes inside, and all those other things your busy point of view character isn't going to do, or is doing quietly, internally. Some books have more narrative exposition than others. Part of what makes a book a "fast-paced page-turner" is a focus on staying in scene and the relative lack of narrative exposition. That said, all stories require narrative exposition. There is no escaping it, no matter how fast you'd like to pace your book.

Narrative exposition is often the best tool for providing the reader with backstory. It functions by slipping outside of the action on the page and focusing the reader's attention on something else, something that is currently relevant, though not current.

Have you ever been driving and thinking about anything other than the act of driving? If your character is driving, the in scene action being performed by the character is driving the car. Through narrative exposition and point of view, you have the ability to leave the act of driving and take the reader on a side journey. Keep in mind, the side journey must be relevant to the present action.

Let's create a scenario using narrative exposition as a vehicle for backstory.

> Snow covered the fields lining the road, and the sun wouldn't be up for over an hour yet. The Ford Focus, an economy rental, was comfortable in an economy sort of way. Mark couldn't get his phone's Bluetooth and the car's stereo to connect, so he'd been driving with just the noise of his tires on the road for company since he left the metro over an hour ago. The coffee he bought at the airport was giving him a stomachache. A garment bag hung in the back seat with a black suit in it. He didn't know if he'd put the suit on. It could be overkill out here in the sticks. Or it could be expected by the farming crowd, always more traditional and more conservative than he could stand. The rotgut caused by the airport coffee only got worse the closer he got to his boyhood home. A home he hadn't seen since the day his old man ran him off with a shotgun in hand. Mark slammed on the brakes. The rental stopped quicker than he expected, and Mark lurched forward, his seatbelt locking across his chest, then pinning him to his seat. He fumbled with the latch, released the belt buckle,

and finally threw open the door. Mark tumbled out of the car onto the gravel road and vomited the remains of the coffee and a breakfast burrito.

Did you notice the backstory? It's this: A home he hadn't seen since the day his old man ran him off with a shotgun in hand. One sentence of narrative exposition reveals the source of this story's tension and indicates that Mark's claim that the coffee is upsetting his stomach is false. His stomachache is caused by his anxiety about going home, which is revealed in the single line of backstory.

FLASHBACK

Flashback differs from narrative exposition in that you shift from the present action to past action, moving from one scene to another. In a flashback you show action in real time as it is happening, except you and your reader understand that you've moved back in time to reveal the past.

Let's look at the example with Mark, this time putting the backstory into a flashback.

Snow covered the fields lining the road, and the sun wouldn't be up for over an hour yet. The Ford Focus, an economy rental, was comfortable in an economy sort of way. Mark couldn't get his phone's Bluetooth and the car's stereo to connect, so he'd been driving with just the noise of his tires on the road for company since he left the metro over an hour ago. The coffee he bought at the airport was giving him a stomachache. A garment bag hung in the back seat with a black suit in it. He didn't know if he'd put the suit on. It could be overkill out here in the sticks. Or it could be expected by the farming crowd, always more traditional and more conservative than he could stand. The rotgut caused by the airport coffee only got worse the closer he got to his boyhood home. A home he hadn't seen since the day his old man had run him off with a shotgun in hand.

Mark lifted the screen door as he opened it so the hinges wouldn't squeak. "Early to bed, early to rise" had long been his parents' motto, which made missing curfew an easy temptation to satisfy—so long as he didn't get caught sneaking in. He stepped over the threshold into the house, turned around, and carefully shut the door behind him. They never locked anything, living way out in the boonies like they did. It took twenty minutes on the best day just to get into town. That seemed justification enough for staying out late, gallivanting around, as his mother liked to say. Mark put a hand against the wall to steady himself and reached down with his other hand to unlace his sneakers. His mother had a shoes-at-the-door policy that didn't apply to his parents. He'd stopped questioning such inconsistencies long ago.

Mark turned away from the door and crept toward the staircase. He put a hand on the banister, a foot on the first step. A light snapped on in the living room.

Mark's father sat in the green recliner—he'd turned it around to face the entryway—with his shotgun across his lap. His cleaning kit sat open on the side table, under the lamp he'd just turned on. Mark's heart caught somewhere high in his chest. The cleaning kit seemed like a prop, a ruse, to avert suspicion for an act that had yet to be committed.

"'Night, Dad." He turned to face the stairs, lifted his foot to bring it to the next step.

"Is it true?"

"Is what true?" His voice sounded small. It was the voice of an intruder.

"I heard the things some of the boys said about you, but I did not want to believe them. And then Dale..." Dale was a mean old gossip. If someone's troubles weren't big enough, Dale could be counted on to exaggerate them into fact. "He said he seen you coming out of a deer blind with that Johnsen kid."

"We were just having a beer, Dad. Shooting the shit and getting messed up. Like you and Dale do every Saturday." Mark clenched the handrail and looked up, hoping to find a saving grace at the top of the stairs.

"Thing is, Dale had his binoculars on him. He saw you. He saw what you did with that Johnsen kid."

This was possible. The blind they'd chosen consisted of a frame draped with camouflage netting. It belonged to Mark's cousin, and he was at work. It was also, they had thought, set away from the most-used trails. Count on Dale to come trudging through their part of the woods and to not leave well enough alone.

His father rose from the chair and came toward Mark, the shotgun in his hands. The natural thing would have been to set it down, lean it against the chair or the wall, but he hung onto it, held it across his chest like he'd been taught in the army. Ready, aim, fire came all too easily to this man. Mark rocked on his feet, uncertain which way to go. Should he launch himself up the stairs, deeper into his father's house? Or hurl himself backwards, at the door and the world outside?

It had turned out it wasn't Mark's decision to make; his father had had a plan.

Mark slammed on the brakes. The rental stopped quicker than he'd expected and Mark lurched forward, his seatbelt locking across his chest, then pinning him to his seat. He fumbled with the latch, released the belt buckle, and finally threw open the door. Mark tumbled out of the car onto the gravel road and vomited what remained of the coffee and a breakfast burrito.

Did you catch the signal to the reader that we were about to enter a flashback? In a flashback the reader goes back in time to live the event the character is currently remembering, processing, or otherwise coping with, even subconsciously. The flashback is written as though it is the present time, but it is framed by signal sentences that let the reader know where the flashback begins and ends.

The past perfect or past perfect progressive tense is typically used in these signaling phrases: had + past verb or had + been + -ing. It had rained all day. They had sung together in the choir. She had been attending college when the trouble began. They had been fighting a lot in those days. Using "had" more than a few times is awkward and should be avoided. Limit the use of the past perfect tense to one or two instances at the open and close of the flashback.

In the example above, the first signal sentence is: He *hadn't* seen it since the day his old man *had* run him off with a shotgun in hand. This is a past perfect sentence that introduces the flashback to come, while connecting it to the current action. The second signal sentence is: It *had* turned out it wasn't Mark's decision to make; his father *had* had a plan.

You might be able to get away with not using the past perfect tense. It depends on how clear your transitions are. Verb tense, however, is a convention to help you create a sense of time in your writing. The past perfect tense indicates an action in the past that is completed before another action begins. Your entire flashback scene began and ended before the *now* on the page, so the past perfect tense is ready-made for you to convey that to your reader. That's pretty damn cool, so why wouldn't you use it? Conventions, including the conventions of language, are widely accepted and followed, which means your readers will understand without effort.

You can also use formatting to offset flashbacks from the main scene. Simply use a line of whitespace between the main scene and flashback. While not required, it creates a visual cue for the reader, further marking the transition for the reader.

A NOTE ABOUT FLASHBACKS: THEY DO NOT COME OUT OF THE BLUE

Unlike narrative exposition and dialogue, flashbacks, due to the time travel component, require a prompt. In the Mark example, the entire scene is a prompt for the flashback. He is driving home to his father's funeral, so it is natural that he is thinking about the last time he saw his father. Sometimes, however, you want to introduce a flashback in the midst of action that seems unrelated. In that case, the flashback needs to be triggered with an object or a sensory cue—something the character sees, hears, smells, touches, or tastes.

Suppose Mark is at work, settling into his desk, a fresh cup of coffee steaming before him. What would cause him to remember his father kicking him out? His phone might ring. He picks it up, intending to silence it, but sees it's his friend from home. They haven't had contact in a few years at least, so he answers. His friend tells him the news: his father has died. The friend adds that he's sorry Mark had to find out from him. That phone call will introduce intrigue: why is Mark learning of his father's death from a friend he hasn't spoken to in years? Who else should Mark hear it from? Family, presumably. So why isn't he getting a call from his mother? It is only natural that, prompted by the emotional news of his father's death, Mark remembers the last time he saw his father.

Sometimes the prompt needs to be subtler than a phone call. Say you want your character to remember playing with her brother when she was a kid. She's walking through a parking ramp and a flash of copper catches her eye. She bends down to pick up a penny. It's been flattened into an elongated oval. This one came out of one of those machines that flattens the penny while stamping something on it. The stamp is for a train museum.

Finding a penny in a parking ramp is a common, but random, occurrence. Because you bothered to include it in your story, it must be significant. The significance? That lies in the flashback.

With the penny in hand, your character remembers the summers she and her brother spent in the country with their grandparents. A train track ran through a field behind the house. She and her brother liked to collect pennies and lay them on the tracks, then wait for the trains to rumble past. They ran with the engine as long as they could, pumping their arms overhead to ask the conductor to blow the whistle.

That's a happy memory, but in most stories, flashbacks are connected to some wound the character carries within. That wound will be a motivating force in either a positive or negative way in the *now*-story, and it must be significant to the character's now. In our example, perhaps the brother was later hit by a train.

The trigger might be a sensory experience, instead of an object. Hearing a popular song on the radio is not interesting, unexpected, or significant, but if your character is walking down a city street and hears a busker playing a twenty-year-old song that he danced to with his high school sweetheart, it's likely to prompt memories.

When you are deciding what to use to trigger your flashback, make sure the object or experience is interesting, unexpected, emotional, and significant.

DIALOGUE

Putting backstory into dialogue can be a great way to let the reader know what's going on. You never have to leave the present moment if your backstory is in dialogue. You also don't have to leave the current action. You stay *in scene* and do not slip into narrative exposition when you reveal backstory through dialogue.

The pitfall with using dialogue for backstory is that some writers try to disguise *telling*, a weak narrative style, by putting it inside quotation marks. Having a character speak the words is no excuse for telling.

Here is the example again, this time using dialogue to reveal the backstory.

Mark stood in the doorway, a glass of wine in one hand, a small paper plate in the other. Several cubes of cheese skewered with ruffled toothpicks sat on the plate alongside baby carrots and a dollop of Ranch dip. One of the ladies had brought the coffee urn and old Correlle dinnerware over from the church. The dishes were plain, sturdy, never in fashion, but never out of fashion. So humble and homely and durable. His mother sat on the other side of the room, a coffee cup and saucer on her knee. The white glassware against the black of his mother's dress drew the eye right to it, like a beacon. His mother lifted the coffee cup to her lip and he watched her hand tremble slightly. *Is it grief or old age?* he wondered. And then he wondered if there was a difference.

When everyone except his mother's friends had gone, she left her seat on the sofa and set down her coffee cup. She walked across the room, her body heavy, and placed a hand on Mark's shoulder. "I never understood why you left, Mark, but it's good you came home." She patted him and slipped through the doorway into the dining room.

"You..." He turned to face her as she moved away from him. The kitchen doorway was on the other side of the room and the faucet was running, the women in there speaking in hushed voices. "You never knew why I left?"

She put a hand on the back of a chair and turned to face him. "No. I never knew where you were, so how could I ask?"

"Did you ever ask Dad?" Mark took a step toward his mother.

"No." She dropped her head.

"Why not?"

"Mark..."

"Why not?" He spoke loudly and more emphatically than he'd meant to. The voices in the kitchen went quiet.

She pushed a hand into the curls on her head and sighed. "He would have told me if there was something I needed to know."

"That's it?" He crossed the space between them and grabbed her hands in his. She flinched as he raised their hands between them. "I'm your son. Your only son, and you never asked the *one* person who knew something about it what had happened or where I'd gone."

"Mark, I..." She pulled her hands free to clutch the chair back, the flesh around her nails turning white from the pressure she exerted. "I thought you didn't want to be found."

"Did you ever try? I kept a listed phone number, Mom. All these years. I kept a landline when everyone else was getting rid of them, just so I'd be in a phone book somewhere."

She lifted her head and met his gaze. "Well, I never moved, Mark. I've lived my whole entire life right here." Her finger stabbed toward the floor beneath her feet. "You didn't even need a phone book to call me. The number hasn't changed in fifty years." Her voice became a quiet screech. "If you wanted me to know how you were doing, *you* could have called *me*."

She was right. Mark counted up the years, the way his life had changed, how many times he could have simply picked up the phone. He knew his father's routine, the ebb and flow of life on a farm. Every day there were bankable times when he could have found his mother at home and his father away. Mark had been so angry. As the anger released, oh so slowly over the years, something else crept in. Apathy. It became easier to pretend he had no parents, that his mother had known and been complicit, than to make any effort.

The women in the kitchen had been quiet for some time. Even the water wasn't running in the sink. Perhaps they dried the dishes softly with their tea towels. Perhaps they had snuck out the back. Perhaps they were listening intently.

Mark reached toward his mother. If he could feel her warmth again he might make it right. She slipped her hands into his. They were still soft. She had remained thin when so many women around her grew plump and flabby. Her hair had been so dark when he last saw her. Now it was a stunning silver mane. His imagination placed her in the city with him. He put her in Bermuda shorts, a short-sleeved plaid blouse, and sandals, her hair in a bun. She sat on a bench, watching the sunset over the ocean, and laughed at the newness of the world.

"Did you know?" he asked, and looked into her eyes, so dark, so sad. "Did you know that the night I left, Dad ran me off?"

"Mark," she whispered, "your father was a hard man, but he wasn't a bad man."

"Did you know?"

"He loved you so much."

Mark shook his head.

"He did, but"—tears began to flow down her cheeks—"you became the one thing he couldn't understand. The one thing."

Mark flung her hands away. He realized suddenly that he glared at his mother, in her funeral dress and her pearl necklace, the most precious piece of jewelry she owned. He turned his head to stare instead at the crocheted curtains over the window. His great-grandmother had made those curtains as a girl for her trousseau, countless hours with a bone crochet hook, turning fine yarn into long panels of diamonds and flowers. Such flimsy things, yet they might as well have been the bars of a prison.

"Mark. I always knew what you were. And I knew that your father couldn't stand it." She hammered back her emotions. "You had so much confidence. And anger, too. I knew you'd land on your feet, would be better off away from here." She raised a hand to touch his cheek. "And look at you now. So strong. So successful."

Mark turned his face away from her touch. "Did you know he had his shotgun that night? Did you know he ran me off with his *gun?*"

His mother's hand fluttered away from her side, reaching again for the chair back. It did not find it and she sank to the floor, her skirt crumpling around her folded legs.

In this section of the Mark story, I reveal in his dialogue with his mother that he was run off with a shotgun. If I were to use this passage, I might place the flashback after this scene or not use it at all. The important moment here is the reveal when Mark tells his mother *and the reader* that his father had a shotgun that night. His mother's reaction, crumpling to the floor, shows us that she did not know. What's more, her shock indicates that this news is a revelation for her, and revelations change our characters' lives forever.

TO EXPOSE, TIME-TRAVEL, OR SPEAK?

Which technique to use depends on:

- how important the moment is to your present action,
- how much the scene reveals,
- your pacing for the scene, and
- what kind of impact you want the reveal to have on the characters.

As we saw in the Mark story, using **narrative exposition** can effectively hint at the reveal, keeping much of the action for later. It's a good way to quickly insert information about the past without removing us from the present action. Also, the pace of the scene is not slowed and it's easy to create intrigue by not giving away too much.

Using **flashback** is often the most impactful way to show backstory. This is because it puts us *in scene* in the action of the past. That moment from the past that is affecting your character now comes to life for the reader. Also, when you're writing in scene, you're showing everything that happened. You can cut the scene off in order to hide something from the reader, but if you're reliving a moment with your character, you cannot keep certain details out of the scene that is on the page. That would be like playing a movie and placing a black bar over half the screen; it cheats your reader. If you aren't ready to play out the flashback in full, use exposition or dialogue.

The drawback of flashback is that it takes us out of the present action. Revealing the past through **dialogue** keeps us in the *now-*story, which can increase tension and *pacing*, the speed at which events seem to be occurring. Possibly the greatest reason for using dialogue to reveal backstory is that, in dialogue, your character must be interacting with another character. Mark could not have this conversation with his mother while driving alone. The impact of the backstory is no longer just between Mark and the reader. His mother's reaction is as important as Mark's. Mark's wound is old and he's been coping with it for years. For his mother, this news creates a fresh wound. Perhaps, knowing now that her husband held a gun while disowning their son forces her to rethink who he was and the choices she made. Not only that, with the women in the kitchen overhearing everything, the effects of this discussion can spiral out into the community. Those impacts are not attainable when the backstory is revealed in exposition or flashback.

If you still aren't sure how to reveal your backstory, grab a journal and freewrite the scene using two or three techniques. One will bring the scene to life in ways the others do not.

EXERCISE 6: THE GREAT WHY OF BACKSTORY

In the previous chapters, you discovered a lot about your character by filling out the Character Building Worksheet. You developed your character's appearance and traits, skills, and life lessons. You also know the premise of your story, if not your plot. Now let's tie those together. You will:

- decide which details from your character's past are necessary to understanding who he is now,
- decide which parts of his past are history and which are backstory, and
- get the backstory on the page for the reader.

Backstory addresses why questions. Each why question raised in the reader's mind increases intrigue. Why is my character the way he is? Why does he do that? Why does he believe this? The reveal provides the answer to the questions being posed, satisfying the reader on that point.

1. In your journal, write down a few things you know about your character's past.

2. For each of those things, write down how it affects the *now-story*. Is it history, shaping the character's worldview? Or is it backstory, necessary for the reader to understand his actions and reactions?

3. For each item you marked as backstory, make some notes about how the reveal will happen.
   - What questions are answered by this reveal?
   - What kind of reveal should it be? A small one or a big, dramatic surprise?
   - Will it be a good source of suspense? Should it be placed fully in one scene, or parceled out over time?
   - Will the repercussions of this reveal affect characters besides the point of view character? If so, how? How can those effects be used to advance the story?

- Which of the techniques for including backstory will have the most impact for this reveal? Narrative exposition, flashback, or dialogue?

4. Practice your backstory skills. Pick one of the items on your list and freewrite for fifteen minutes for each kind of reveal. If you feel stuck, reread the examples of Mark revealing that his father kicked him out of his home.
    - Write the backstory as narrative exposition.
    - Write it as flashback.
    - Write it as dialogue.

5. Make some notes in your journal about this exercise.
    - Was writing one kind of reveal easier or more fun to write than the others?
    - Which reveal will be most effective for this piece of backstory? Why?
    - What else have you learned about backstory by practicing with your own work?

RECAP

In this chapter, we've defined and discussed history and backstory. We've gone over two methods for discovering your character's backstory and three methods for effectively working it into the story.

- History is essential to character development. It is relevant to the story on the page in that it shapes the character's personality, beliefs, attitudes, etc.

- As the writer, you need to know your character's history, though the reader may never know the specifics.
- Backstory is immediately relevant to the action on the page and the reader's understanding of that action.
- Weave backstory into the main story, revealing it as it becomes relevant.
- You can reveal backstory through narrative exposition, which allows the narrator to control how much is revealed when, without pausing the action of the *now*-story.
- You can reveal backstory in a flashback, writing it in scene, which allows the action of the past to be experienced as present action by the reader through the device of memory and time travel.
- You can reveal backstory through dialogue, which allows the backstory to be part of the action of the *now*-story, which maintains or escalates the pace of the current scene. In dialogue, the effects of the reveal can expand to include other characters.
- How you reveal backstory depends on your goals for tension, pacing, and reveals.
- Exercise 6: The Great Why of Backstory. In this exercise, you practice identifying backstory and how it can answer questions about your character, increasing intrigue that builds to a reveal. You also practice incorporating backstory into your *now*-story as narrative exposition, flashback, and dialogue.

Special Section

An Excerpt from M.A. Robbins' *The Tilt*

In this Special Section, we'll examine excerpts of M.A. Robbins' post-apocalyptic western, *The Tilt* to illustrate one use of flashbacks and backstory.

We first meet Jon Streg a decade after a cataclysmic event changed the world as we know it. He's a lawman in a future Wild West version of Anchorage, Alaska. Robbins chose to use flashbacks to reveal Streg's backstory. Doing so, he tells the story behind the story. The reader discovers why Streg is who he is now and how he's changed as a result of past tragedies. The flashbacks create a separate narrative with a separate cast of characters within the main story. The people around Streg in the flashbacks are either now dead or they, like Streg, have been changed by the events of the apocalyptic event, known as the Tilt.

Through the flashbacks, Robbins unwinds Streg's past while moving the reader forward to his present. By parceling out the backstory into short episodes, he creates suspense. This suspense, however, is not for the *now*-story. It's for the backstory, a self-contained journey closely related and relevant to the *now*-story.

In this first excerpt, we meet Jon Streg for the first time. This is the opening scene of the book.

CHAPTER ONE

Jon Streg field-stripped two Glocks, a .45 caliber slimline and a .40 caliber full size, cleaned them, and placed both on the table. A wallet-sized picture lay between them, taken and laminated back when such things were possible. He stroked the photo where Rachel's hair flowed around her shoulders.

She smiled at the camera as if stifling a laugh, but in reality she'd been pissed because he'd just told her pictures were a waste of time and money. He'd wanted them taken with a phone camera, but she insisted on having them done professionally.

"Becky will love looking at them when she's older," she'd said. "She'll get a kick out of seeing her mom and dad when they were young."

His eyes drifted to the gap made by the finger missing from his left hand. The ring finger. He'd lost both the digit and the ring together.

He moved his forefinger over to the image of Becky, tracing the outline of her gap-toothed smile. She hugged her stuffed tiger to her chest. He'd gotten it for her because it was her favorite cartoon character. What was its name? Delbert? Dingo? Yes, Dingo the Tiger.

Between them sat a stranger, looking nothing like the man he'd become. No pain in his eyes, no fear, no hatred. His face had no hair, no scars. A young smartass. Streg hated him for what he had in his arms.

The gas lamp guttered and broke his concentration before flaring back to life. The tiny room on the second floor of a former pawn shop had become his self-imposed prison the past two days. The bed with its rusted springs made sleep impossible for more than a couple hours. Since he'd about run out of whiskey, he couldn't even make it that long.

Black-out curtains covered the windows. Nothing to tell the outside world the building was inhabited. He sat on a chair next to the only other piece of furniture, a rickety desk.

Picking up the photo, he kissed it twice, once for Rachel and once for Becky, and placed it in his left shirt pocket. Pain seared his gut. If Rachel had listened to him about having the picture taken, he would've forgotten how they looked.

He picked up the .45. His favorite. Never missed a kill with it.

He reassembled it in seconds, popped in the magazine, and jacked a round into the chamber. Out of habit, he ejected the magazine and topped it off with another round.

Closing his eyes, he pressed the cold barrel to his temple. The gun dipped slightly. Did it get heavier or did his wrist muscles give away his fears?

I'll be with you soon.

His finger tensed against the trigger. He didn't want to mess this one up.

A rustle outside. He stopped. Opened his eyes. He pointed the gun toward the door and listened. In Old Anchorage, most buildings were uninhabitable. No neighbors to worry about.

A thump. Someone on the stairs. He moved to the bed and covered the door at an angle. A stair squeaked, the third one from the top. Not heavy enough to be a man. Animal? Too furtive.

"Son of a bitch," he said, then yelled, "What do you want, kid?"

Silence.

"I know it's a messenger boy out there. Which one is it? Henry?"

A squeaky voice replied, "Yes, sir."

"That's 'Yes, Judge.'" He stepped to the door.

"Yes, Judge."

"You'll get yourself shot sneaking up my stairs. Next time call out and let me know it's you."

"Yes, Judge."

"What the hell do you want? I'm busy here."

"TBone told me to—"

"That's Ranger Tosi to you." The words were automatic on Streg's tongue.

"R-ranger Tosi said he needs you at Red's Inn, Judge."

"What for?"

"He didn't say. Just that it was urgent." The boy paused, then added, "Judge."

Shit!

If TBone didn't come himself, then he had a damn good reason. As many times as he'd saved Streg's life, how could he leave him hanging? More than just Judge and Ranger, they were brothers.

Rachel and Becky are waiting, too.

"Judge?"

"Shut up, kid. I'm thinking."

A soft thump came from the stairway. The kid must've sat down, probably too afraid to leave until told to do so.

Streg had already failed Rachel and Becky. He could never undo that, but he could help TBone.

Studying the gun in his hand, he no longer had the nerve or the liquid courage to finish what he'd started. Maybe someone would finish the job for him. It hadn't happened yet, but it might. Maybe tonight. He could only hope.

But he'd make sure the kid's odds were better. "Henry?"

"Yes, Judge."

"What're you carrying?"

"My mother's .38."

"You can't hit shit with that. Get up here."

The boy clomped up the stairs, the sound of his heavy breathing seeping through the door.

Streg fished a shotgun and shells out of the closet. While the gun had a crack in the stock in the shape of a "Z," it was still a serviceable and deadly weapon. He eased the front door open. No one out there but the boy. Henry jumped when Streg stepped into the hallway, eyes avoiding contact. He became a statue, as if one wrong move would give Streg cause to blow him away.

Streg opened the bag hanging from Henry's shoulder and stuffed the shells inside. A single drop of sweat slid down the boy's face, leaving a trail through the dust caked on his cheek. His close-cropped red hair glistened in the gaslight.

Streg thrust the shotgun into Henry's hands. "Take this. There's a shell in the chamber. These streets are no place for a lame .38."

Henry took the shotgun and held it as if it would be snatched back any second. The damn gun was as long as he was. Friggin' kids were either tough or worm bait in Anchorage. There was no middle ground.

Henry broke into a wide grin. "Thanks, Judge." He sprinted down the stairs.

Streg shoved the .45 into the concealed holster on the right side of his pants and let his shirttail drop over it. After reassembling the .40, he jacked a round into the chamber, topped off the magazine, and holstered it cross-draw on his left. Throwing on an old wide-brimmed panama hat, he hurried out the door.

Following the path of intermittent gas lamps through Old Anchorage, Streg scanned the shadows. Sounds of movement echoed from the ruins. Animal or human, the skulking didn't signal friendly intent. Fog had rolled in from the inlet, reducing visibility. Ripe weather for an ambush. He pulled the .40 and held it at the ready.

A cloud of his breath blew past his cheek as he walked at a hurried clip past the skeletons of the old world. Probably the coldest temperatures for winter, maybe somewhere in the fifties. It hardly compared to pre-Tilt Anchorage.

As he came within sight of New Anchorage, the number of gas lamps doubled, forcing the shadows to recede. Traffic increased and the fog began to dissipate. Pedestrians stayed to the side to avoid being run over by bicyclists and horses. Each traveler carried a visible weapon: a pistol holstered to a hip, a rifle slung over a shoulder. All gave him wide berth, except some drunk sailor probably trying to find his way back to the docks. He weaved toward Streg, singing off key in some Asian language. Others on the street stopped and watched. Streg sensed their anticipation.

Almost certainly a harmless drunk, the man would probably end up walking into one of the bottomless rifts that crisscrossed the city, remnants from the Tilt. His shipmates would leave without trying to find him. It wasn't unusual for a sailor to disappear once they left the docks.

Still, he might be a clever assassin or a young jackass looking to make a name for himself by lulling Streg in with his act, then pulling on him when close enough. There'd been more than a few who wanted "I killed Jon Streg" etched on their tombstones. They all got the tombstone part.

Streg raised the gun and fired in one motion. A clump of road exploded between the drunk's feet. The man fell backward in surprise and struggled to get up. Nothing clever about that one, just drunk on his ass. Streg holstered his gun and picked up the pace. TBone waited.

He approached Red's Inn from the alley. It was a crappy '70s one-story motel that had escaped major damage during the Tilt. The alley ran along the rear of the inn where each room had a back door. The front doors faced the road and broken sidewalk. As he neared the inn, Streg caught movement in the shadows to his right and reached for his .40, but a hand the size of a catcher's mitt clamped down on his and held it fast. He pulled back, but it was like trying to remove his arm from hardened cement. His kick to the shadow's groin was blocked, and a smiling face the size of a watermelon emerged from the darkness.

"Hi, Boss."

"TBone, you big friggin' monster. How can you sneak up on me like that?" TBone stood at least two heads taller than most men and was built like a bull.

The ranger kept his smile, but released his grip. "Dunno." His wavy hair, which he inherited from his father's Samoan side of the family, spilled out from under his pork pie hat and down his shoulders. A scar ran from the left corner of his mouth to his ear, making his smile look unnaturally wide and lopsided.

"What's the emergency?" Streg asked.

TBone's smile faded. "Californian." He nodded toward the inn. "Room eight."

Streg's heart skipped a beat. Now this was something worth interrupting his night.

This second excerpt occurs in chapter seven, over forty manuscript pages after the first chapter. At this point, we have a solid understanding of who Jon Streg is and what he's doing now, but we don't know who he was before the Tilt or what made him the way he is now. That is what the flashbacks are for.

Here, we have the first flashback, in which we glimpse Jon Streg before the Tilt.

ANCHORAGE, ALASKA
TEN YEARS EARLIER

Jon took his time, allowing the hot water to stream down his back. The bathroom still smelled of lavender from Rachel's bath earlier that morning. He wasn't expected in the office until ten, and as an extra bonus, he'd miss rush hour traffic. It surprised him the lawyers let him off easy, since they considered paralegals little more than servants.

He threw on the suit Rachel had left out and opened the shades. The sunlight left shadows over the corners of the apartment building's backyard fence, allowing small piles of snow to survive another day. Everything else was painted a montage of green and brown, tantalizing hints of spring.

As soon as he opened the bedroom door, the sizzle and smell of fried bacon overwhelmed him. Rachel was still there? The TV blared from the living room. Puzzled, he plodded down the hallway to the kitchen. She should've already been at work after dropping Becky off at school.

"Good morning, Daddy." Becky sat at the table, blue eyes gleaming.

"What's my punkin still doing here?" he asked. A half-empty bowl of cereal sat in front of her. "Careful you don't spill milk on your school clothes."

"Mommy's sick, and I'm late for school."

Rachel leaned against the counter, dressed in an old sweatshirt and pants. Her hair fell over her face as she cut a sandwich in half and sealed it in a plastic bag. "I think I caught your bug, Jon."

"Daddy made Mommy sick," Becky sang, tilting her head side to side in rhythm, her blond ponytail swishing back and forth.

Jon leaned over and tickled her until she nearly fell off the chair. "And who made Daddy sick, wiggle worm?"

"Me!" Becky said, giggling.

"You should've kept it," he said. "You're not supposed to give me presents until next week."

Becky held up two fingers on one hand and all five on the other. "You'll be two five years old, Daddy."

"Twenty-five," he corrected. He helped her straighten in the chair before tickling her again, turning her face red.

Rachel placed a plate of bacon and eggs on the table at Jon's seat. "You two need to behave. Jon, let her eat."

He gave Becky his best stern face. "Finish your breakfast, young lady."

"I want a good morning kiss, Daddy."

"I'd kiss you, punkin, but I don't want to make you sick again."

She swung her spoon around, flinging a drop of milk across the room. Her voice went up an octave. "I don't care, I want a good morning kiss."

"If I make you sick, you'll look like Mommy. You don't want to look like Mommy, do you?"

Becky laughed. "No way." She dug into her cereal.

Rachel mouthed the word "asshole" to him. He winked and blew her a kiss.

"I'm taking her to school then going back to bed," Rachel said. "I already called in sick."

He encircled Rachel in his arms from behind. "Why don't you go to bed now? I'll take Becky. I've got time."

She turned and put her arms around his neck, laying her head on his shoulder. "Thanks. That'd be great."

She grew heavy against him, and he pressed a hand to her forehead. "You're really hot, honey. Come on. To bed. I'll finish putting Becky's lunch together." He guided her toward the hallway.

"No." She stopped and veered back toward the kitchen. "I want to at least see her off."

Rolling his eyes, Jon sat at the table and ate a forkful of eggs. "What's on the tube?" He pointed the remote at the TV and turned the volume up.

Becky cried, "Cartoons!"

He flipped through the channels, stopping at the image of a middle-aged man standing behind a podium. A cluster of microphones crowded its surface. His gray suit and red tie gave him an air of authority.

Camera flashes painted his face and shoulders. Lettering at the bottom of the TV screen identified him as Dr. Barry Jelinek.

Becky whined. "Not news. Cartoons."

"Just a minute, punkin." Jon scooted his chair around to see better.

Jelinek spoke. "We've been on a historic journey to change our world as we know it. Geothermal energy promises clean, renewable power for a fraction of the cost. It's been our driving force the past fifteen years."

He paused, looking directly into the camera. "Two years ago, as we were on the cusp of realizing this dream, the federal government pulled our funding. Their alarmist rhetoric about the safety of our plans also dried up any private capital. But we wouldn't be denied. A statewide referendum to fund our research was passed by ninety-five percent of the California voters." Applause erupted and he nodded.

Off camera chanting broke in. "No injection! More protection!"

Jelinek's smile faltered. The TV cameras swung to show a small group of protesters waving signs and tussling with security guards in back of the crowd.

One protestor broke away and ran toward the podium. The camera tracked him. A guard caught up with him a few feet from the stage. The older man, long gray hair in a ponytail, screamed, "You can't inject into a fault line. You'll kill us all, you fool." Spittle flew from his mouth and he continued yelling while the guard dragged him off.

The camera swung back to Jelinek, and he picked up where he'd left off. He was a cool one.

"Twenty minutes from now, we'll inject water into the chamber to build up pressure using the patented Jelinek process, and within a month we'll be producing over fifteen thousand megawatts, far more than all the current US geothermal output combined. Electricity that will power our economy well into our children's futures."

More applause.

A short, dumpy man in a white lab coat tapped his shoulder. Jelinek leaned over, and the man whispered in his ear. Jelinek nodded and held out one finger to the man.

He waited for the applause to die, a dazzling smile painted on his face. When the last clap faded, he leaned forward. "Dr. Meese has reminded me of our schedule, but I would like to leave you with a thought. As our governor so eloquently put it when the funding bond passed: 'As goes California, so goes the world.'"

Jon turned off the TV.

Rachel placed a cup of coffee in front of him and sat down. "California's been giving out IOUs instead of checks the past few years and they could fund this?"

He took a sip of coffee, savoring the taste. "If it hits big, the state gets a chunk of the profits."

"Daddy, what's a megawatt?" Becky asked.

"A lot of electricity, punkin."

"Oh." Becky played puppets with her two pieces of toast.

Rachel wiped her forehead with the back of a hand, her blue eyes bloodshot. He put his arm around her. "Seriously, honey, you need to get to bed."

She rested her head on his shoulder. "I feel so shitty."

"Mommy said a bad word." Becky wiggled a finger at her.

Jon chuckled. "We've got to get going. You're already late for school."

Caressing Rachel's face, he leaned in to kiss her. She jerked away. "Not on the lips. You'll get sick again."

He kissed her on the cheek. She gave him a smile, the corners of her lips rising and falling so fast he almost missed it.

Becky climbed out of her chair and grabbed her lunchbox from the counter. She stopped and kissed her mother on the cheek. "See you later, alligator."

"After a while, crocodile," Rachel said as she hugged her.

Notice how different Jon Streg is from one scene to the other. Also notice the importance of Becky to each scene. Questions are raised in chapter one that are just beginning to be answered in this first flashback. It's no coincidence that they have the news on the television in this scene. A character critical to the *now*-story, Jelinek, is introduced in that broadcast in a subtle fashion. We also learn something about Californians here.

The flashback scenes that come later in the book have to do with how Jon Streg survived the first days of the Tilt, how he lost Becky, and how he came to be a ranger. Robbins made sure each flashback is gripping in its own way and also relevant to the action surrounding it.

Find out about M.A. Robbins at the back of this book.

Chapter 6

Secret Agent Man

THE SECRET POWER OF AGENCY

I spout lots of rules, but I also tell writers that the only *real* rule in writing, my cardinal rule, is: You can do anything you want, so long as you do it well.

Well, there's an exception to the cardinal rule. You must not ever, under any circumstances, write a passive protagonist. To write a passive protagonist is to commit a sin against all Story.

In honor of the cardinal rule, let's just say I can't imagine anyone successfully writing a story with a passive protagonist, because it would be a boring story. If you want to prove me wrong, go for it. If you do it well, and have the sales record and reviews to prove it, let me know. I will revise the above edict. It's more likely, however, that I'll point out that your protagonist is not actually passive.

If you aren't to ever write a passive protagonist, you must write an active one. That is, a main character who has agency.

You've no doubt heard that you need an active protagonist. An *active protagonist* is one with agency. *Agency* means your character actively makes choices throughout the story, takes action, consciously reacts to the consequences of those actions, and ultimately has control over her own fate. In the next chapter, we'll explore the forces that motivate your character to choose and act.

It often appears as though a character does not have control over her own fate, even to the Puppet Master…I mean, writer. By the end of this chapter, you'll know how to ensure your character has agency, despite the cruel twists of fate and machinations of your antagonist.

WHAT'S CHOICE GOT TO DO WITH IT?

If stuff is happening to and around your character, you're writing a *passive protagonist*. Your protagonist must be active, not reactive. He must shape his own destiny. That means making choices, right and wrong, one after another, and facing the consequences of each.

The issue of agency can become confusing when we look at all the things that happen in a story. Many of them come from outside your character and, therefore, happen *to* him. If that is the case, ask yourself if your character has *reacted* to or *responded* to the situation. Reactions are passive; responses are active. Ask yourself if he had a choice in the situation and if his action propelled the story forward. If the answer is yes, you're fine. The choice might be as simple as controlling his temper or letting it fly. Letting his temper get the better of him is a choice that leads to an action that leads to a consequence. And *that* is what we are looking for: choice, action, consequence.

Sometimes the villain seems to be running the show. This is true of most crime stories. If the protagonist is in pursuit of the antagonist, the antagonist will seem to be the one making all the choices, performing all the actions. It's one thing for the protagonist to be the cat in a game of cat and mouse, but it's another thing for her to *only* follow the antagonist's lead. Make certain your protagonist is faced with decisions to make, and that she makes them—for better and worse!

Agency is about the hero making
choices and taking actions
that lead to consequences.

To figure out whether a character is active or reactive, let's look at how a character moves through a story. Here's a summary of a story:

- Joe went for a country drive.
- A UFO appeared over the road.
- Joe was beamed aboard the ship.
- Joe was probed.
- Joe's memory was erased.

- Joe was returned to his car.
- Joe was unconscious until morning when a police officer found him parked in the middle of the road.
- Joe went home.
- Joe went to work, but he couldn't focus because he kept having visions of strange lights.
- Joe was yelled at by his boss and sent home.

Pause here to assess the summary you just read. What do you think of it?

I think it's boring. If a summary of your character looks like this, you'd better be worried. Of course, you probably have lots of great specific detail in your mind to fill in the gaps, but that's no excuse. No story summary should look like this. Whether you write the summary for yourself, your query letter, your editor, or your back cover, it should make clear the protagonist's role in the action.

That summary does make clear Joe's role in the action, doesn't it? His role is to be there while things are done to or around him.

Let's try it again.

- Joe takes a country drive to clear his head after another argument with his ex-wife about their son's belligerence.
  - Joe's drive is purposeful, not random. We immediately understand something about his life and his troubles. A choice precipitated this drive. He could have stayed home, gone to a bar, called a friend . . .
- As Joe crests a hill, a large, triangular, black UFO rises before him. He slams on the brakes and stares through

the windshield, not believing his eyes. The craft hovers, perfectly still. It must be fifty feet across with glowing lights at each corner and another in the center. It rises higher, then zips out over a field of half-grown corn and hovers near the center of the field, like it's waiting for Joe.

- – This is the inciting incident, something happening to Joe that he didn't invite or control. The question is, how will Joe respond to this event? He has a choice: get the hell out of there or investigate.

- Joe climbs out of his car, leaving the keys in the ignition. He stares over the roof of his car at the ebony triangle suspended over the corn. The corn isn't even waving; there's no sign of engines or fans or any kind of mechanical propulsion.

  - – This passage will up the tension by showing more of the UFO and its strangeness. The reader expects something to happen, and this is the moment of anticipation.

- Joe steps off the road into the field. He begins walking toward the craft, not certain why, but he needs to see it up close. As he moves through the field, he realizes it's silent— no grasshoppers, no bats, not even a breeze rustling the stalks of corn. Joe begins to run toward the craft.

  - – Joe has taken action. He made a choice and moved of his own volition.

- Joe wakes up when a sheriff's cruiser bleeps its warning horn at him. He looks around from the driver's seat of his car. It's dawn. There's a fog over the fields on both sides of the road. A farmhouse and barn dot the horizon before

119

the road curves to the east. Joe's mouth is incredibly dry, practically glued shut. He rubs his eyes as the sheriff taps on his window. The sheriff asks if he's aware that he's parked in the middle of the road, a winding county road with a speed limit of fifty-five? He's lucky the sheriff was paying attention when he rounded the last curve. Joe pushes the door open and tumbles out of the car to vomit on the pavement. The sheriff assumes he managed to stop and turn off the engine before he passed out drunk, then slept off a bender in the middle of the road. Joe yells at the sheriff to leave him alone. He says abusive things that don't make sense.

- Joe yells at the sheriff. Maybe something happened to cause him to lose control, but maybe he's fully aware of the fact that he's shouting at a law enforcement officer. Either way, he is acting and the sheriff will have to respond to him. Joe's action will have consequences that will—if properly written—escalate the story's rising stakes.

- Joe is arrested and taken to the county jail. He calls his ex-wife to come bail him out.

  - Here Joe is dealing with the consequences of yelling at the sheriff, and he has a choice of whom to call. We know his relationship with his ex is strained. If he calls her, it further develops that subplot. Now he'll have to face her anger and shame. He'll have to explain himself to his son or try to hide it from him. Joe could call a lawyer or a friend. This could be a good time to introduce another supporting character. Whomever he calls, it has to factor into the plot and subplots. Joe might not remember the UFO now, but he's got to get himself out of a mess. If he pulls out a credit card and walks out of the jail on his own, the consequences are limited to his own consciousness and any legal record of the arrest. But if he has to seek help, now his issue is known. Any time you bring other characters into the trouble, you complicate it. That's a good thing.

You might be thinking that there are nuances here, that Joe didn't make a choice every step of the way. For instance, he didn't choose for the sheriff to turn up. True. Your character will face many circumstances out of his control, but he will have to respond to them all, and the resulting choices *are* in his control.

Joe did not have to follow the UFO into the field. Joe did not have to yell at the sheriff. Joe probably could have found someone else to call. Whether Joe yelled because he was out of his mind, or because he has a problem with authority, or because his life is at a new low and he's looking for trouble is something we'll have to discover as we develop his character and the plot.

Your character's agency is a combination of Choice – Action – Consequence. If you aren't sure what choice your character should make, write it out.

EXERCISE 7: THE AGENCY TREE

When in doubt about what your character should do to most effectively move your story forward, make an Agency Tree. If you're working on a story now, choose a situation that has given you some trouble or a scene you doubt is at its most impactful. If you aren't currently working on a story, choose one of your past characters or invent a new one and a situation. You don't need much to get going.

If you like, write about a woman named Karen who lives in a midsized city. Karen's biking home along a trail. The bike and pedestrian traffic have thinned to almost nothing, because the sun has set. Her chain falls off the gears and jams up the pedals. Now her rear wheel won't turn. She forgot to grab her cell phone when she left home in a rush. She's not in a bad part of town, but it could be questionable, especially after dark. There you go: a character and some trouble.

1. Write your character's name and the situation at the top of your journal page.

2. Write out each of her possible choices for what to do about the situation.

3. Below each possible choice, write out the complicating factors.

   → If one of Karen's choices is to start walking, a complicating factor is her bike. With a wheel that won't turn, her bike won't exactly roll. Is she going to drag it home? How far away is home?

4. Below each complicating factor, write down any subsequent complications.

→ If Karen starts dragging her bike home, how long can she go before she's tired and frustrated to the point of giving up?

→ If she drags her bike, would she stay on the now-deserted trail, or look for populated streets and help?

→ If she looks for help, whom will she meet first? Will she approach this stranger or keep looking?

5. After you've made your Agency Tree, follow the chain of possible consequences from each choice your character makes. Choose the most interesting, compelling choices all along the way.

Lots of interesting things can happen *to* our characters, but we need our character to *do* interesting things. Doing is about making choices, which is the character's agency. As you examine your Agency Tree, keep that in mind. It's not a see-what-happens-next tree. It is a decision tree, and I'm calling it the Agency Tree to help you keep your goal as the writer in mind: create a character with agency, an *active* protagonist.

If Karen chooses to wait beside her bike and see who happens along, that's a passive choice. Don't do it. Have your character make a choice that leads to action. Have that action lead to consequences.

By making an Agency Tree, you've examined all the possible choices your character can make and the resultant consequences of each one. Often, we stick with the first idea that comes to mind and write our story from that one moment. The first idea is not always the best. The Agency Tree helps you discover stronger choices. They should not be easier for the character. We want difficult, complicated choices that raise the stakes for the character and increase the dramatic tension for the reader.

Let's examine the steps in Joe's Agency Tree. Each numbered item is followed by three possible actions Joe could take, signified by the arrows. The best choice is played out in the next numbered item. If you create an Agency Tree in your journal or on a paper napkin, it could look like this.

1. Joe goes for a country drive and a spaceship appears over the road.
   → Grab his phone and call 911.
   → Stop the car and watch.
   → Drive away.
2. Stunned, Joe stops the car. The UFO zips out over a cornfield.
   → Get his phone and record things.
   → Get out and follow the UFO.
   → Wait inside the car.
3. Joe follows the UFO into the field. Next thing he knows, a sheriff is tapping on his car window. He has no idea what happened between chasing the UFO and now.
   → Apologize and hope the sheriff lets him go home.
   → Act belligerent and irrational.
   → Explain to the sheriff what happened and hope the sheriff doesn't think he's crazy.
4. Joe's arrested by the sheriff, who is not amused by Joe's behavior or his story.
   → Call a friend or attorney.

→ Call his ex-wife.

→ Pull out a credit card, pay a fine, go home.

5. Climactic scene: Here we see the consequences of all those choices. This is a chapter-level climax, not the book's climax.

→ Joe tells his ex about the UFO and she goes ballistic, accusing him of being mentally ill or on drugs. She threatens to keep him away from their son.

You can easily see that at each juncture in the story, the character has a choice. Pick the option that is the result of your protagonist's agency *and* will lead to more *trouble*. If Joe pays a fine and walks out of the county jail, there are no consequences from his arrest. While that is a "nice" choice, it's not a good choice. After you've made your Agency Tree, go back to a choice near the middle or beginning and pick a different option. See what would happen to the chain of events that follows if you try something else.

Once you bring other characters into the scenario, they have choices to make as well. Each choice will affect the chain of events for your protagonist. Joe's ex could tell their son that Joe is crazy, in an attempt to turn the son against Joe. His son could support him or withdraw from him. Either way, Joe has a new set of troubling circumstances to respond to, which is the source of forward motion in a story.

You can go to www.WordEssential.com/ JoinStoryWorks to receive a downloadable and fillable Agency Tree. The download includes instructions and a new example, as well as a blank tree you can print and use every time you need to structure a scene around your character's agency.

RECAP

- Agency is about creating an active protagonist, one who makes choices that shape the story by getting himself into and out of trouble throughout the story.
- If you aren't sure if your protagonist is active, create a summary of the story, focusing on the character's role in each scene. You should be able to spot whether things are happening to and around him or if he's actively choosing, acting, and responding.
- Exercise 7: The Agency Tree. This exercise helps you ensure your protagonist is active and helps you find the most compelling course of action to move her through the story to the climax.

Chapter 7

But...What's My Motivation?

GIVING YOUR CHARACTER DRIVE

What motivates your character is the desire to experience some and avoid other reactions or consequences. You know all about this, because it's as true for you as it is for your character. You exercise to avoid a heart attack. You study to avoid failure. You work to gain experiences that you value. You work to avoid being poor. This is often referred to as the pleasure principle, the instinctual seeking of pleasure and avoidance of pain.

Your character's motivation is
the desire to achieve some and
avoid other consequences.

WHY DOES YOUR CHARACTER NEED MOTIVATION?

It's easy to see why you need to give your character motivation if you look at your own habits and patterns. What do you do when you are motivated? Read *War and Peace*. Run a marathon. Roll five kinds of sushi. Clean your entire basement. And when you aren't motivated? Sit on the couch. Watch television. Crack open another beer. Lie in bed. The motivated protagonist is an active protagonist. An active protagonist is crucial to any story.

It's not enough to decide your character is going to be motivated. You need to know what motivates her. This connects motivation to the pleasure principle. What does she *want*? The wanting of something, whether to gain or avoid, launches every story. Jess wants to put her ghost to rest and not be haunted. Jon Streg, the ranger in M.A. Robbins' *The Tilt,* wants to complete his final mission and retire.

The thing the character wants is her goal. The goal motivates her to take action. That action will have a reaction. Every choice the character makes along the path to achieving that goal will have a consequence.

No story is as straightforward as goal identified, goal accomplished. We expect our characters to suffer between the identification and the accomplishment of the goal. This is where obstacles come into your story.

THE GOAL–OBSTACLE– MOTIVATION TRIFECTA

For every *goal*, there is an *obstacle*...or twenty. These obstacles are the challenges your hero faces on the way to realizing his main goal. Goals and obstacles exist on two levels: plot and character.

The **goal-obstacle pairings in plots** are easily identified, because they are tangible objectives that often center on physical objects. These are "get the treasure" and "save the world" goals. Opposing forces battle for the goal. The opposing forces are typically driven by opposing characters. Even when they want the same treasure, you must view the struggle from the protagonist's perspective, because that is the character the reader empathizes with. Thus, the protagonist wants the treasure, and the antagonist wants to keep the treasure from the protagonist.

In *The Murder in Skoghall,* the protagonist, Jess Vernon, wants to save her house (goal) from the ghost who is haunting it (obstacle).

In M.A. Robbins' *The Tilt,* the protagonist, Jon Streg, accepts a mission to track down a spy (goal) plotting to destroy his homeland (obstacle).

The **goal-obstacle pairings related to our characters** are less easily identified, because they are intangible and relate to motivation. Understanding why we do things is usually a complex, fuzzy question. Knowing your character's motivation to pursue her goal begins with who your character is, including the history that has shaped her.

Imagine a three-layer cake. It represents the levels of your character's motivation. To illustrate, we'll look at both *The Murder in Skoghall* and *The Tilt.*

Top Layer:

This is the **surface motivation** that is apparent to the writer, character, and reader. Everyone can readily identify this motivation, because it tends to be simple, tangible, and obvious on the page. Money and duty are just such obvious motivators.

Why does Jess want to save her house from the ghost? Because she just sunk her divorce settlement into this place.

Why does Jon lower the gun and accept a new mission? Because it's his duty and his friends need him.

Middle Layer:

This is the **psychological motivation** that lies beneath the surface. It is apparent to the writer, reader, and possibly the character, if he's introspective. The source of this psychological motivation is typically found in the character's backstory.

Jess, being newly divorced, is grieving the loss of her marriage and home. She's creating a new life for herself and isn't willing to be driven away from another home.

Jon has failed loved ones before, and carries terrible guilt over that failure. He can't abandon people he loves when there's a chance he could help them.

Bottom Layer:

This is the **overarching motive,** a **driving force** that compels your character to keep overcoming obstacles in pursuit of his goal. It is buried in the character's psyche, and is known by the writer and possibly the reader. The character is generally unaware of this deep psychological drive, becoming aware of it—if at all—as it's finally resolved at the end of the character arc, when the character's evolution has come to fruition.

For Jess, it's the need to live her life on her own terms.

For Jon, it's the need for redemption.

We're taking big bites here. This bottom layer is the force behind the force. When you get into your character's overarching motivation, the one that drives the book or series, you'll discover something about your character he doesn't realize himself, something connected to the work's theme. *Theme* is that intangible something that your story is about, such as grief, love, power, or the cost of success. It defines the primary issues your character will struggle with over the course of the character arc.

Jess won't live life on her terms—home or not—until *she is able to have faith in herself.*

Jon won't find redemption through the mission or the love of a woman until *he forgives himself.*

This bottommost, deep-seated, psychological motivating force is connected both to the theme and to the character's fatal flaw.

PUTTING IT ALL TOGETHER

We're wise to remember Newton's third law of motion: For every action there is an equal and opposite reaction.

What is story, but the movement of a character through a series of dramatically compelling events? To apply Newton's law to story, you must keep in mind that every one of your character's actions will have a reaction, and when an action happens to your character, your character must have a reaction.

Simply put: action—reaction or choice—consequence.

This plays out in every story as the protagonist faces an obstacle, overcomes it, and then faces another, greater obstacle, until finally vanquishing the foe. In these examples, you can see that everything the protagonist does leads to a new, more difficult obstacle, which he now must address.

Action: Jess chooses to stay in her house.
Reaction: The ghost escalates the haunting.

Action: Jess brings her boyfriend home.
Reaction: The ghost possesses her boyfriend and he attacks Jess.

Action: Jon Streg puts the gun down and answers his door.
Reaction: He's assigned a new mission.

Action: Jon Streg spends the night at his girlfriend's bar.
Reaction: Mercenaries set fire to the bar.

As the obstacles grow in difficulty and consequence, motivation is the force that keeps the protagonist engaged.

If a character's motivation is weak, the reader will sense it. Motivation is the glue that holds the story together, keeping the protagonist in the game as stakes rise and he has more and more to lose.

> Every step of the way, ask yourself
> why your character doesn't just
> walk away. The answer will be
> found in his motivation.

If your character has a family and the family is being threatened, a logical reaction would be to take the family and leave the conflict. Your character must prize her family. If she doesn't, the threat to them is inconsequential and therefore not story-worthy. If your character prizes her family, she will be motivated to protect them. The easiest way to protect them is to leave the conflict. What motivates her to stay in the conflict *despite* the threat to her family? That is the question you must answer to hold your story together and to hold your reader's attention.

When a character's motivation keeps her in the conflict, despite the best, easiest, most logical other option, you've got a story with the forward momentum of *inevitability*. Inevitability is the sense that this is the only reasonable course of action, despite the obstacles, and it will pull a reader through to the climax. Without it, the protagonist will no longer seem credible, the events no longer plausible, and the story will fall apart.

> You must know and demonstrate your
> character's motivation in order to create
> a sense of inevitability that will keep
> the character (and reader) engaging
> in increasingly difficult conflict.

EXERCISE 8: BAKE YOUR MOTIVATION CAKE

You've seen how your character's motivation is layered, like a cake. To work through your character's motivation, ask yourself what keeps your character in the game, despite mounting hardships?

1. Write down the general idea behind the climax of your story. You don't need to have all the details, just a sense of what your character will face. In the case of *The Murder in Skoghall,* I could write: Jess has to relive the ghost's murder in order to finally find the evidence that clears an innocent man's name.

2. Make a list of what your character stands to lose over the course of the book. I might write down: friends, dog, home, money, life.

3. What is the surface motivation that keeps your character in the conflict? For Jess, it's financial.

4. What is the psychological motivation that keeps your character in the conflict? For Jess, it's because she can't stand to lose another home.

5. What is the driving force that keeps your character in the conflict? This is the motivation that is connected to your theme and your character's fatal flaw. For Jess, it's the desire to live her life on her own terms.

6. Make some notes about what you've just learned about your character and his motivation. Knowing his motivation, the force that keeps him in the game, will help you create the

sense of inevitability that makes even the toughest, craziest choices seem reasonable.

RECAP

In this chapter, we've examined your character's motivation and how it creates compelling forward motion.

- Story depends upon your character moving through a series of dramatically compelling events.
- Your character must act and react to each obstacle he encounters while in pursuit of his goal.
- Your character's actions are always motivated by a driving force that is complex and layered.
- The top layer is apparent to the writer, character, and reader.
- The middle layer is apparent to the writer, reader, and possibly the character, if he's introspective.
- The bottom layer is buried in the character's psyche, and is known by the writer and possibly the reader. The character is often unaware of the deep psychological drive, becoming aware of it, if at all, as it's finally resolved at the end of the character arc.
- Exercise 8: Bake Your Motivation Cake. In this exercise, you examine your character's motivation in order to understand and better create inevitability in your story.

Chapter 8

Supporting Characters Can Save Your Story

THE MANY USES OF CHARACTER-DRIVEN SUBPLOTS

Being human is about relationships, which is why there are so few stories about hermits. Your main plot is about the action of the story, but your subplots are about your character's relationships. It's here she gets to make a mess, struggle to be a better person, and generally live her life. In your subplots, your protagonist engages with your supporting characters. And sometimes, supporting characters get to take the spotlight. *Subplots* are narrative threads that showcase your character's life and the themes of your work. And every book-length work of fiction needs one or several.

137

Readers can get futuristic gizmos, ripped bodices, time travel, or mustachioed black hat villains in any number of stories. What will make a reader loyal to your books are your characters. Subplots make them real, sympathetic, troubled, complex human beings. While your FBI agent is tracking the serial killer across state lines, she can be lamenting the fact that she hasn't been home to tuck her son into bed for the last six nights. Plot: agent after a serial killer. Subplot: the trials of being a working mom.

You don't want to be wholly defined by your day job, and your character doesn't want to be wholly defined by her main plot. Use subplots to give your character room to breathe, kiss, fight, and grow as a human being.

> The plot is where your character gets to be a hero. The subplot is where she gets to be human.

LOVE YOUR SUBPLOTS (AND SUB-CHARACTERS) AS MUCH AS YOUR READERS DO

When you give your character a full life, you need supporting characters who fulfill certain roles in that life. Your character and the supporting characters will share all kinds of moments that make your story richer. Put time into your supporting characters and their roles. In doing so, you'll find it easy to develop your subplots around your main character's relationships. Subplots are critical to propelling your character through the story and to making readers care about the character's life. To illustrate this, let's look at the plot and subplots in *The Murder in Skoghall*.

I've had the chance to talk to some readers of my Skoghall Mystery Series at book clubs and author events. I've heard from them that it's my characters that keep them engaged with the story. The message I'm getting is that while my main plot, the haunting, is well constructed and fun, at the end of the book, readers want to know what will happen with Jess, Tyler, Beckett, Isabella, and even Shakti, Jess's golden retriever. That's exactly what I want to hear. As the author, I enjoy writing the mysteries and ghost stories, but it's the characters that keep me coming back to that world, book after book. The reason these characters engage both me and my readers is because they have fully developed roles in Jess's life—in other words, they have meaningful subplots.

> Your supporting characters can
> make or break your subplots
> and, therefore, your story.

Here's a list of my subplots and the supporting characters involved in them.

- Main plot: Jess's house is haunted by the ghost of Bonnie who was murdered there forty years ago.
- Subplot 1: Newly divorced, Jess hits the dating scene with "interesting" results, first with Tyler and then with Beckett.

- Subplot 2: Beckett and Tyler have a romantic rivalry for Jess's affections.
- Subplot 3: Besides the ghost in her house, Jess discovers the spirit of a young girl, Isabella, haunting an antique store.

Notice that each subplot features supporting characters. In fact, those subplots would be impossible without the supporting characters. The ghost in the antique store, Isabella, is a case in point. She has a small role in the book. My intention is for her to add a quirky character to Skoghall and to show that Jess's new psychic ability isn't limited to her personal ghost—that there might be more to her new gift. When I ask readers if they have a favorite character or someone they really want to see in future books, they say Isabella.

This shows that a well-developed secondary character can turn into a scene-stealer. This is a good thing, because your readers' reactions will help you shape that character's role in the next book. I had already planned to include Isabella in book two, but it's good to know that she's one reason readers will return to Skoghall. Her role in book two is still small, but I did expand it from book one. I also ended book two with a *hook,* an unresolved question that indicates her role will continue to expand in book three. I mention her in the sales copy as well, because readers will be looking for her.

Isabella is a hit with readers, because she is a fully formed character. I gave her backstory and personality and intrigue. I took the time to make her real. Just because a character's role is minor, doesn't allow you to skimp on her development.

In this brief excerpt from *The Murder in Skoghall,* Jess and Isabella make their introductions.

Jess parted the dresses on their hangers and revealed a girl of about seven years. "Hi," Jess said.

"Hello." She looked at the floor. Jess followed her gaze and watched as her right foot swiveled away from the left, nervously tapping to the side three times before resting next to its counterpart. The small feet were shod in scuffed black boots with low heels that laced up the front, and the girl was wearing white stockings, despite the heat, under a dress that fell below the knees. The girl lifted her chin to look at Jess with incredible green eyes. "My name is Isabella. I'm not supposed to introduce myself to grown-ups. Only Mama or Papa is supposed to introduce me around. But they've been gone an awful long time. I think we would never know each other's names if I continued waiting for them to make us acquainted."

Take the time to properly develop your supporting characters, and readers will reward you by caring about them and wanting more.

SUPPORT AND COMPLICATION ARE NOT MUTUALLY EXCLUSIVE

Look at your own supporting characters and their roles in your main character's life. Note that supporting characters are often supportive of your main character and her goals, yet they complicate the protagonist's life. A complication creates tension, which is a good thing in fiction. *Tension* is what the reader feels when there is an unresolved question implied by the story, both through the action and the relationships on the page.

Consider the young apprentice who has a limited amount of time to train with a master in order to become fit for battle or competition. The master dictates the apprentice's schedule, diet, etc. The master annoys the apprentice with his authoritative presence and repetition of drills. The apprentice must learn to obey the master. As the apprentice evolves, he also learns to appreciate the master's wisdom. The master-apprentice relationship is a character-driven subplot, and the master is wholly supportive of the apprentice's goals. The complication has more to do with the main character's resistance than the master's methods. The tension arises from the question in the reader's mind: will the apprentice mature and develop the necessary skills in time to defeat the villain?

Tension between supportive characters can be delightful. If you've read L.M. Montgomery's *Anne of Green Gables,* you know that Marilla is Anne's supporter. Marilla is a hardened spinster at the beginning of the book. She takes in the orphan, Anne, with great misgivings, but out of a kind heart. Marilla also disciplines Anne and humbles her, making her apologize when she offends the neighbor. Marilla rolls her eyes aplenty at Anne's folly. The tension between these characters originates in the contrast between their personalities. The question raised by this tension is, Will Anne soften Marilla, or will Marilla constrict Anne's spirit?

SUPPORTING CHARACTERS AND THEIR COMPLICATIONS INCREASE TENSION

Let's look at my Skoghall Mystery Series, books one and two, to further understand the complications and tension that arise from supporting characters and their involvement in the story. First, I name the character and subplot. Second, I describe the complication. Third, I ask the question implied by the complication, which raises the story's dramatic tension.

- Isabella's subplot is about Jess's developing psychic ability. She tricks Jess into bringing her home, giving Jess more spirits to deal with. Will Isabella help or interfere with Jess's life?
- Beckett's subplot is about Jess's romantic life. He helps her a lot, but it takes time for him to accept her gift, which makes it harder for her to accept it. Can Jess work with her ability *and* have a relationship?
- Investigator Martinez's subplot is about Jess's involvement in murder investigations. Just when Jess thinks she's done with ghosts, Martinez asks her help him with a case, drawing her back into working with killers and victims. How will Jess cope with violence and sadness? Can she walk away from it?
- Shakti's subplot is about Jess's home life and responsibility to others. Shakti is used to lure Jess into danger. Will Jess save Shakti in time? How will she and the dog change after this experience?

I realize you don't know who all these characters are. That's all right. What's apparent is that these supporting characters, Jess's friends and loved ones, each in their own way make her life more complicated, strengthening the story through engaging subplots, and raising dramatic tension by implying questions that keep the reader engaged.

CHARACTER-DRIVEN SUBPLOT OR SOGGY MIDDLE? NOT A DIFFICULT CHOICE

I hear from writers that they fear the *soggy middle* problem. That's when your characters have to do a bunch of boring legwork or are waiting around between the inciting incident and the climax. As a result, the tension drops and readers start thinking about naptime. These writers aren't sure how to get around the problem, and they're afraid of losing readers in the middle—rightly so. Avoiding the soggy middle isn't hard, *if* you make good use of your supporting characters. As we saw in the above section, supporting characters keep the tension up where it needs to be to keep your reader engaged.

In Judy K. Walker's, *Braving the Boneyard,* Private Investigator Sydney Brennan has to do lots of research, paperwork, and door knocking to unravel her case. That's normal for any mystery. (I sat Jess down in a library with a microfiche machine in *The Murder in Skoghall.*) Being still and gathering data aren't unique to mysteries, though. Lots of books contain what I call "traveling chapters," that's when your character needs to get from A to B. The reader has to know the distance was covered for the rest of the book to make sense.

That A to B could be logical legwork, like in a mystery, or geographical legwork, like in an epic fantasy.

Say you've got a situation like Walker and I have, where your character isn't going to get to the end of the story without a traveling chapter or two, how do you avoid the boredom of the soggy middle? Here are some tips to help you keep your readers engaged.

- Make the setting and tertiary characters interesting. If you're having fun with the old Carnegie library and its staff, your reader is more likely to enjoy the setting too. If your elfin barkeep is a great storyteller, the journey will be more entertaining.

- Keep in mind that the reason you're making your character do the legwork is because it will reveal something important on the road to the story's climax. Reveal enough during the chapter in question to raise the intrigue, but not enough to spoil a big reveal later.

- Use your supporting characters and subplots. Sydney Brennan, Walker's private investigator, was attacked in a previous book and she now has PTSD. Sydney coping with a past trauma is a character-driven thread through the story, a subplot. I advised Walker to introduce situations that force Sydney to deal with her PTSD in that middle chunk of the main plot, when she's doing a lot of grunt work to get to the bottom of her case. It helps make Sydney a real person with real problems.

> Involve the reader in the scene
> by asking him to invest in the
> character's personal issues.

Remember, subplots, like backstory, work when they are intrinsic to the main plot. If Sydney's PTSD makes it hard for her to confront some aspect of her job, we have a solid relationship between the character-driven subplot and the action-driven main plot. Jess's romantic involvement with Tyler brings him into her home, where her ghost is able to possess him, which both complicates her romantic life and dramatically escalates the haunting.

Weave your subplots and your plot together so they have a complicated, oftentimes causal relationship. In doing so, you'll avoid the soggy middle, because when your main plot gets a bit slow, the subplots will maintain the tension and rising stakes that keep your reader interested in your character, who is (you'll remember) the heart of your story.

INCREASING TENSION BY PROMOTING A MINOR CHARACTER

Sometimes the answer to avoiding the soggy middle is as simple as promoting a minor character into a bigger role. I often see manuscripts in which there's a minor character who's ready-made to complicate the protagonist's life in a well-developed subplot that will increase tension and ensure readers don't doze off during a traveling chapter.

In D.J. Schuette's thriller *Chaos*, his main character, Nick, is practically estranged from his mother. She lives out of state and only serves to introduce backstory. Nick and his mother annoy each other over the phone; as such, her role is minimized and ineffective. (Our characters need to use the phone sometimes, but phone calls are not powerful on paper.) It is harder to create conflict when the other end of the conversation is far away. I suggested Schuette bring Nick's mother to town and get that conflict on the page to strengthen the subplot. This developed the relationship between the characters, increased tension, and helped avoid the soggy middle.

If you think you've got a soggy middle *and* those traveling chapters are essential to the cohesiveness of the whole, turn to your supporting characters. Don't overlook the minor ones. Ask yourself, how can this character get more involved in my protagonist's life, thereby complicating her story?

EXERCISE 9: DEVELOPING YOUR SUPPORTING CHARACTERS AND SUBPLOTS

In this exercise, you'll make a list of your supporting characters and explore how they can best be used to engage your main character and your readers with subplots that raise tension, while avoiding the soggy middle.

1. Make a list of your primary supporting characters. They're the people involved in your main character's life: family, friends, colleagues, etc. Note: the antagonist, your

character's nemesis, is not one of the subplot characters. He's all about the main plot.

2. Write down each supporting character's role in the main character's life.

    – Is this character a help, distraction, or hindrance to the main character's goals?

3. Add notes about how each character can be involved in the story in a meaningful way.

    – In what ways could this character complicate the main character's life? Think about all the aspects of life: home, work, romance, material wealth, spirituality, etc. Remember that a supporting character's subplot does not have to be antagonistic to the main character to complicate the story. In order to complicate the main plot, a character might need to be manipulated a little by the hand of the author. Craft your supporting characters' backstories and roles in ways that allow for the most effective subplots to support your theme.

4. See if any of your minor characters are not being used effectively. Go back over your list and try to enhance each character's role.

    – Write notes about scenes that could dramatize the subplots for each of these characters. Turn those ideas into action on the page. Here, go for bullet points or rough sketches. Then see which notes get you excited. Those are the subplots to focus on.

5. What questions are implied by the supporting characters roles in your protagonist's life? How do those questions raise the tension for your reader?

    –   Write out those questions and make notes about how to best incorporate them into your story.

Turn off your inner critic and let the ideas roll out! When you're finished, you could have something like the list of my Skoghall Series supporting characters, their subplots, how they complicate Jess's life, and the questions implied by those relationships that raise tension and keep readers interested.

I hope you surprised yourself as you uncovered the potential for new threads to weave through your story, complicating your character's life and enriching your reader's engagement.

RECAP

*   Subplots are character-driven, thematic threads through your story.
*   They grow from the relationship between your supporting characters and your main character.
*   Use your supporting characters and their relationships to your protagonist to prevent the soggy middle.
*   Creating tension through supporting characters and subplots can open new possibilities for your main character.
*   Exercise 9: Developing Your Supporting Characters and Subplots. In this exercise, you explore your supporting

characters' roles and how you can use them to create dynamic subplots.

Excerpts from Judy K. Walker's *Braving the Boneyard* and D.J. Schuette's *Chaos*

In this Special Section, we'll compare excerpts from both early drafts and revised or published drafts from two books, looking at characters and subplots. In both excerpts we're concerned with the characters' personal lives.

JUDY K. WALKER'S *BRAVING THE BONEYARD*

In this scene from the original draft of the book, Private Investigator Sydney Brennan is sitting in a clerk's office, examining a gun that is evidence in the case she's working.

At this point, if Trevor denied supplying the gun, it was his word against Jerome's. I didn't like those odds, so I needed to connect the gun to Trevor, corroborating Jerome's story while preferably keeping Jerome off the stand. The gun wasn't exactly a gangbanger's first choice—it didn't hold enough ammo and it didn't look particularly badass. The wooden grip showed enough age to make me think it had been tucked away somewhere for years, only occasionally brought out rather than used (or displayed) on a regular basis. In his deposition, Trevor had said he had no siblings and no father in the picture, that he and his mother lived alone. The gun could have belonged to her.

I opened my eyes and realized my thinking and gun fondling had drawn a few stares. In particular, a chunky guy in need of a haircut looked like he was just waiting to be a hero and take me down. I smiled and gave a little wave, before remembering I still held the gun in my hand. Perhaps it was time to leave the clerk's office.

This is a traveling scene, getting Sydney and the reader from A to B. In this case, the distance is logical. She's working through the connections between the evidence and the suspects. Closing her eyes and "fondling" the gun is amusing. The scene, however, does not have a lot to recommend it to a reader, beyond the fact that it contains information necessary to understand who did what to whom.

In this published version of the scene, Sydney is again sitting in the clerk's office with the gun.

> The revolver wasn't exactly a gangbanger's first choice—it didn't hold enough ammo and it didn't look particularly badass. The wooden grip showed enough age to make me think it had been tucked away somewhere for years, only occasionally brought out rather than used (or displayed) on a regular basis. In his deposition, Trevor had said he had no siblings and no father in the picture, that he and his mother lived alone. The gun could have belonged to her.
>
> *Or it could have belonged to a man in the dark. A man waiting to kill you.*
>
> My eyes flew open and I saw the gun was shaking. Correction: my hands were shaking. The gun was just hanging out in them, as guns do, waiting to be used. Another tremor ran through me, one so violent that I dropped the gun on the table. My poor gun-handling skills drew a few discreet glances. One heavyset man (whose hair had apparently been cut by a barber as palsied as I was) stared intently, as if he were just waiting to be a hero and take me down. What did he think I was going to do, throw

the gun at him? The way my pulse was racing, I just might. I stumbled past a security guard and fled toward the exit.

In this revised scene, the reader gets the necessary information about the case, the "traveling" from A to B. But the reader also gets so much more. Walker uses Sydney's PTSD to enrich this scene with more meaning and tension. The reader is no longer just a witness to Sydney's detective work; the reader is engaged with her emotional state and invested in the scene.

In this scene, Sydney is talking about the case with a colleague. She has a faded black eye.

I gave him the broad strokes without going into any confidential details. I still felt an emotional hangover from dealing with Jerome. "I'm not sure a woman investigator is the best fit for this guy," I admitted. "I think you could have gotten more out of him."

"Maybe," Mike said. "But the investigation isn't just about dealing with him. In fact, it's mostly *not* about dealing with him."

The waitress came with a split check and we pulled out our credit cards. It was cheap, probably because the primary ingredient in everything they served (bright yellow cheese) was inexpensive. As was Lucifer's tea. Mike glanced at his watch.

"Damn. I've got to get back for a team meeting. But before I do, is there anything you want to tell me?" He opened his eyes wide and fluttered his lashes. I was at a loss. Finally, he squinched up one side of his face like a paralytic pirate.

I laughed. "I'm afraid I was a little too enthusiastic in my self-defense class."

In this early draft, the characters are talking shop. It's useful information for the reader, but not exactly compelling fiction. Perhaps the most interesting part of it is the joke about cheap yellow cheese. When Mike references her black eye, Sydney laughs it off.

Here is the published version of the scene.

I gave him the broad strokes without going into any confidential details. "The trial date's coming up fast, and I'm feeling the pressure." Not to mention still feeling an emotional hangover from dealing with Jerome. I admitted, "I'm not sure a woman investigator is the best fit for this guy. I think you could get more out of him."

"Maybe," Mike said, crunching next to me. "But you know as well as anyone that early visits are pissing contests. It sounds like you're holding your own. And the investigation isn't just about dealing with him. In fact, it's mostly *not* about dealing with him. Don't let it get to you."

I nodded and tried to smile. "You're probably right."

Mike washed down his chips with a swig of beer before turning his full scrutiny on me. "This isn't like you. You're a damned good investigator, and you know it. What else is going on?"

He was right. I might not have a clue about most things in my life, but I know my job. I'm good at it, and I didn't want my twitches and nightmares interfering with that. "Probably just tired," I said. "I haven't been sleeping well lately."

"Your lack of sleep wouldn't have anything to do with *this*, would it?" He opened his eyes wide and fluttered his lashes. I was at a loss. Finally, he squinched up one side of his face like a paralytic pirate.

I laughed without experiencing a face twinge, but I should have known Mike would notice the residual hints of bruising. "I was a little too enthusiastic in my self-defense class."

Note in this scene that Mike expresses concern, not just a passing interest, and Sydney is no longer glib. Now the scene has some tension, because we understand from the subtext that Sydney's work is being affected by her PTSD. The comment about twitches and nightmares suggests she's suffering more than she'll let on. In the first draft, her remark about her self-defense class reads like a facetious and disposable one-liner. Here, however, it reads like a half-truth. *Something* happened in her class that shouldn't have, or she wouldn't have a black eye, and she's not going to tell Mike about it. In this scene, it is no longer disposable; it is reason for concern, encouraging the reader to engage with Sydney on a deeper emotional level.

These excerpts from *Braving the Boneyard* illustrate the power of a subplot, especially during traveling scenes. The revisions are not extensive, but the impact on readers' emotions is. We now engage with the scenes on multiple levels, finding ourselves concerned about Sydney's well being while we learn more about the case.

Find out about Judy K. Walker at the back of this book.

D.J. SCHUETTE'S *CHAOS*

In this early draft of *Chaos*, Nick delivers news to his mother over the phone in these two scenes.

Nick hoped for voicemail, but it apparently wasn't his night. He tried to hide his disappointment, but a sigh still escaped him. "Hey, Mom."

"Nicholas?"

Nick rolled his eyes. "Is someone else calling you Mom these days?"

"Don't be a smart-ass. I'm just surprised to hear from you. Your calls are a rather extraordinary occurrence."

That was perhaps a new speed record for the guilt phase of their conversation.

He chose to ignore the jab. "How are you?"

"Oh, I'm dandy. How about you? How is my little crime fighter?" It was impossible to miss the sarcasm.

Nick had long ago resigned himself to his mother's disapproval of his decision to follow in the footsteps that had led to his father's death. On a purely psychological level he even understood her feelings, but it certainly didn't make his conversations with her any damn easier.

"Great. I'm in Virginia for a few days. I was asked to teach a course at the Academy." He hoped it would ratchet down any potential for conversation about him being in the line of fire.

"How nice," she said. The awkward silence that followed indicated her complete disinterest in hearing anything further about his career. "So, am I going to see my son and daughter-in-law at some point before I die, or is that too much to expect from the two of you?"

Nick tried to keep his cool. He closed his eyes, took another deep breath and released it slowly.

"Are you still there, Nicholas, or did you hang up on me again?"

It was amazing, Nick thought, that this woman could so easily annihilate the composure of someone with a psych degree.

"I'm here. Actually, I was thinking that a visit might be a good idea." *No, no I wasn't.* "Connie's pregnant. You're going to be a grandmother."

There was a pause while she processed the news. Nick reveled in the brief ceasefire.

"Hm. Well, I suppose that's a relief. I was beginning to wonder if that would happen in my lifetime either. How far along is Constance?"

Nick bit the inside of his cheek to keep himself in line. After all, he wouldn't want to ruin the best conversation they'd had in years.

"Uh, about sixteen weeks we think."

Wait for it...

She took an insulted tone that was only marginally better than her usual condescension. "So did you lose your phone for two plus months, Nicholas? You didn't think to call me before now? You didn't think this was a bit of wonderful news that I should be privy to?"

Nick fought the urge to ask if she'd been taking her medication. Instead, he sighed again, this time plenty loud enough for her to hear. "No, Mom. We just wanted to get beyond the first three months before we started telling everyone. Just in case, you know?"

"In case what? In case I decided to fly up to Minnesota?"

Oh, sweet Jesus no...

"Not at all, Mom. It's—." He realized trying to explain would just prolong the conversation, or provoke an argument. "Never mind. We were thinking of coming down in a few months."

"Mm. I'm sure," she said in a way that suggested she didn't believe it for a second. "Burt asked me to tell you hello when I heard from you next. He's retiring next month."

Nick heard the barely concealed contempt just below the surface. Even after all Burt and the rest of his father's precinct had done for them throughout the twenty years since his father's death, she still had an axe to grind.

"I'll give him a call later."

"I'm sure you will. I'm surprised you didn't call him first."

Nick ground his molars together hard. "Nope. We haven't told anyone else yet. You're the first to know," he lied.

She sounded skeptical. "How nice."

"We thought so." He couldn't take much more. His head was pounding. "Listen, Mom, Con and I will look into our schedules and vacation time. Maybe we can visit around Christmas. God knows we'd prefer Jacksonville that time of year. Then we can fly you up when the baby is born."

"I suppose that would be acceptable. But right now, it's past my bedtime. Perhaps you've forgotten that I like to turn in at nine o'clock? If you can find time in your busy schedule to call me before my grandchild is born, we can share *pleasantries* then. Good night, Nicholas."

Nick damn near screamed.

"Okay, Mother. Talk soon, sorry about the hour."

She'd already hung up.

"That went well." Nick said aloud as he dug through his toiletry case to find the Tylenol.

* * *

Nick hadn't bothered to call his mother during the surgery. He knew she just would have frustrated him at a time when he was already on edge. Despite many reservations, he supposed he ought to fill her in on the news. The conversation was as pleasurable an experience as he expected.

"Well, that's wonderful. At least now you won't have to come for the holidays," she said.

Her callousness and selfishness drove him into an instant fury, complete with tears.

"Yeah, Ma. We intentionally offed the fetus so we wouldn't have to put up with your impossible bullshit this Christmas. Fuck you!" He hung up on her and resisted an urge to throw his Blackberry at a wall.

An older couple huddled on a couch in the waiting area looked at him with wide eyes then turned away uncomfortably.

Nick rejected his mother's return calls four times before she finally got the hint. He'd have to let that simmer for a while before he was ready to take another bite.

In this revised version, Nick has a different experience with his mother.

Nick and Connie were just sitting down for pancakes when the doorbell rang.

Nick's stomach dropped. "Oh shit."

Connie gave him a withering look. "Who's that?"

He tried to give her a look of sheepish apology, but knew it was nothing more than a wince. "My mother. She wanted to take us to brunch this morning. I completely forgot."

Connie's eyes widened, Nick thought more in terror than anger. The two weren't exactly best of friends. Then again, neither were he and his mother. "Oh, you're really going to owe me for this," she told him.

"Can we just pretend we're not home?" Nick asked.

"As much as I'd like to, no. You go answer the door, I'll dispose of the incriminating evidence."

Nick blew air out of his full cheeks and headed for the door. On the way, the bell rang twice more. Patience had never been among his mother's virtues.

He swung the door open onto a glorious morning, bright with sun and not yet hot.

"Mom." Nick said and grudgingly held the door open for her.

She stepped inside. "Nicholas," she said and tilted her head in greeting. "You're looking well."

"Uh, thanks," he said. "You too." The words came out sounding only partially like a question. This was not the woman he was accustomed to. At least she didn't seem to expect an embrace. He led her in an awkward charged silence through the house to the kitchen. Connie had indeed managed to hide every sign of their near-meal, but the smell of cooked batter was still on the air. There was no way his mother could have missed it, but to her credit she didn't comment on it.

"Constance," she said, the ancient ghost of a smile on her lips.

"So good to see you, Patti," Connie said and stepped forward to embrace her mother-in-law with arms outstretched.

Nick couldn't detect the slightest hint of sarcasm, deceit, or discomfort from his wife. She rarely ceased to amaze him.

"How are you feeling?" his mother asked, her eyes slipping toward Connie's stomach.

"Very well, thank you. My doctor says everything is going smoothly so far."

"That's good." There was a momentary empty pause in which Nick wondered when his mother had been body snatched. "Well, shall we?"

Nick insisted on driving, which gave him something to focus on other than his growing discomfort. Connie managed to maintain a stuttering conversation about nothing during the ride downtown.

After being seated and a few blessedly peaceful minutes of poring over the menu, Nick ordered a Juicy Lucifer, Hell's Kitchen's spin on a Minnesota favorite. Connie chose the lemon-ricotta hotcakes, and his mother decided to take a run at their famous Bloody Mary bar. While she was off building her drink, Nick put his hand over Connie's. "I'm really sorry," he said.

She shrugged it off and squeezed his thumb. "I don't mind. She's actually been very well behaved so far. I'm a little freaked out, to be honest."

Nick gave her a half smile. "You and me both. You don't think she wants to move in with us or something?"

Connie looked horrified. "If she does, I'm moving to Bulgaria with Mindy."

Nick laughed. "I wouldn't blame you."

His mother returned, carefully wielding a glass piled high with pickles, olives, a variety of cheeses, bacon, and other meats. It was a meal in and of itself.

"Good God, Ma," Nick said.

She threw him a sharp look. "No need to take the Lord's name."

Nick bit his tongue and forced himself to not roll his eyes. Next to him he could see Connie's jaw working as she pressed her lips together to keep from smiling.

"There must be a hundred or more garnishes up there. Anything you can fit in the glass, it says. I've never seen anything like it." She slipped an olive off of a toothpick and daintily put it into her mouth.

Nick took a breath and tried to ignore the absurdity of it all. Maybe the liquor would keep her mellow—if she ever made it that far down into the glass.

A polite but harried waiter brought their plates and quickly departed.

"I spoke with Burt last week."

"Yeah, how's he doing?" Nick asked as he cut his burger in half. Cheese oozed from its center like molten, steaming lava. He didn't bother to tell her that he'd spoken to him as well. His father's ex-partner at the Jacksonville Sheriff's

Department had become more a parent to him than his mother had ever been, and they talked often.

"Very well, it seems. He's retiring next year." There was only a hint of bitterness to her tone.

Nick already knew that, but decided not to risk spoiling the conversation or her mood. "He's way overdue. He's been going for what, thirty-five years now?" He took a bite of his medium-rare burger and scalded his tongue on the cheese as it squirted out from the innards of the beef.

"I imagine so, yes." Another pregnant pause as she dunked a bacon strip into her drink and brought it to her lips. "So tell me about what you're doing in Virginia next week."

He had to give her credit. She was trying. Normally, the last thing she wanted to talk about was his job. She had always considered him joining law enforcement as a betrayal of sorts, as if putting himself in harm's way was nothing more than a way to keep her wringing her hands in perpetual anxiety.

"It's really nothing. Orientation on a new system."

"That *you* helped design," Connie said, leaning her shoulder into his. "He's being modest. It's a big deal."

Nick silently wished she'd stop helping.

"That's nice," his mother said, but her interest, as always, was forced.

"Are you excited to be a grandma, Patti?" Connie asked.

Nick was shocked to see his mother's eyes actually light up.

165

* * *

Nick wasn't sure whether he'd rather endure Connie's grief or his mother—neither was preferable to the other—but sooner or later it would have to happen. Nick set his jaw and made his way out to the intensive care waiting area.

His mother stood when she saw him, clutching her hands in front of her. She took a hesitant step forward like she wasn't sure if she should embrace him or not.

Nick saved her the trouble and sat down, keeping an empty seat between them. After an awkward second, she took her chair again.

"How is she?" his mother asked without any of the compassion that a normal human being would convey.

Nick took a deep breath. "She'll be okay."

She shook her head. "What a shame."

Her choice of words set his teeth on edge. He looked at the floor and bit his tongue. "Yes. A *shame*." He wasn't the least bit surprised that she didn't ask how *he* was.

After a quiet moment she looked over at him and said, "I was hoping that the baby might bring us closer together."

As if their baby was nothing more than a means to her end. Anger welled in Nick's chest. His jaw trembled with the effort of holding it in. He turned his face to hers. "I know what you hoped."

Her eyes widened when she saw the hardness in his. "I just meant...I...I'm sorry." It was her turn to look down at the floor. "I guess I don't do grief very well."

"Yeah? You think?" Nick said. She looked back at him. Perhaps for the first time since his father died, he saw a glimmer of real hurt in her eyes. He was satisfied and ashamed at the same time. He sighed. "Look, Mom, you don't need to be here." In fact, he rather wished she weren't.

She regained her usual sharp, sarcastic edge. "Where else should I be, Nicholas? I did just lose my grandchild."

Anger reared in Nick again, irrational and ferocious. "*Anywhere* else, *Mother.*"

She drew a sharp breath. "I—."

"We just lost *our* child. There will be no others. No more chances for you to *fix* us," he hissed. His face felt like it was afire. He threw up his hands. "You can stop trying now."

A few visitors seated in the waiting area got up and found someplace else to be. His mother sat there, ramrod straight, with her mouth partially open in shock. She blinked at him once.

Nick stood and took his phone from his pocket to give himself an excuse to walk away, but his rage wasn't yet spent. He stood over her, looking down into her eyes. "You'll never be half the mother you were before Dad died."

She recoiled as if he'd slapped her.

Nick walked away.

The scenes with Nick and his mother face to face are more compelling, more tangible, and more dramatic. Body language and facial expressions factor in. Setting is depicted. When writing a face-to-face interaction, writers are more likely to flesh out the *scene*, as with the food and the hospital waiting room in this excerpt. The revision of Nick's conversation with his mother after he and Connie lose the baby is highly charged. The image of Nick standing over his mother, looking down on her, is especially powerful, and that could not happen over the phone.

Schuette ramped up the tension when Nick's mom went from a voice on the phone to a character who has presence and impact. That change increases the stakes each time Nick's personal life is on the page.

Find out about D.J. Schuette at the back of this book.

Chapter 9

Got Arc?

WHAT IS AN ARC AND WHY DO I WANT ONE?

Character arc is the evolution of the main character over the course of the story, the process of becoming a different person at the end of the story than she was at the beginning.

Now, why do you need a character arc? Because your reader is rewarded for empathizing with your character by being a part of this change.

At the end of any story, there are two types of payoff, known as *resolution*. One is the plot resolution. When plot is resolved, we are satisfied with how the conflict ended, and we know what happened to wrap up each subplot, whether it's closed or open-ended.

The other payoff, and the one we're concerned with here, is the character arc resolution. When the character arc is resolved, readers are satisfied with the shift that occurs in the character as a result of the events she just endured. Because of the reader's *empathetic connection* to the character, the reader could experience a similar shift in consciousness.

The morality tale provides a good example of how reader empathy works. If the reader of Charles Dickens's *A Christmas Carol* has a strong empathetic connection to Scrooge, he may be moved to greater generosity as a result of reading the story—and all without encountering the Ghosts of Christmas.

No matter your genre, no matter the brevity of your story, you need a character arc in order to move your reader. Readers are moved by the experience of a satisfying change in the character at the end of the piece. To illustrate the importance of moving your reader, no matter your genre or word count, let's look at Ernest Hemingway's shortest story ever. Here it is in entirety.

For sale: Baby shoes. Never worn.

That's right, six words and it's lauded as a complete story. What makes this a complete story? No character is named. No setting is pictured. No dialogue. No action. So how can this be a story? *Who changes?*

The reader creates the character arc and thereby changes through his empathetic connection to the implied characters. The story leaves both the characters and the plot up to the reader to infer. We imagine the parents who bought the shoes, full of hope. Then we imagine their suffering while they write the ad, their grief over the loss of their precious baby, the death of hope. We create the characters who are not on the page and supply the emotion of change, of a complete character arc. And we, the readers, are affected and therefore moved.

As an exercise in understanding what constitutes story and in the power of the reader's imagination, it's an impressive piece of flash fiction. Encapsulating the power of a moment of transformation in only six words is hard to do. Note that leaving so much of the story off the page, for the reader to create in his own mind, only works in flash fiction. If you are writing a short story, novella, or novel, it is your job to create a satisfying character arc that is fully developed and present on the page.

Keep in mind that in a series, you'll want a sense of growth and completion at the end of each book, but there is an umbrella character arc that spans the breadth of books. Only then will the character experience fruition. You'll be wise to have a good sense of your entire character arc before you begin writing, knowing at least the beginning and end points for your character. Know how your character will be a different person at the end of the series than at the beginning.

A satisfying resolution will give the reader a sense of completion and things ending the way they should. This will not necessarily make the reader happy. In *A Stone's Throw,* I kill one of my main characters. No reader has told me the death of the character made her happy, but plenty of readers have said they were glad the character died. There is a certain inevitability about it that makes her death a satisfying character arc resolution.

A satisfying resolution does not necessarily make a reader happy, but it does feel inevitable.

A NOTABLE EXCEPTION TO THE RULE

The exception to this is the charismatic hero of the episodic, plot-driven series. Those books do not need to be read in order, because each book's plot is independent of the others and because the main character does not change dramatically from one book to another. The setting does not change dramatically either. Readers love these books for their dependability: same character, same place, same basic storyline. Sherlock Holmes will forever be a bachelor with an opium addiction, one close friend, and an intelligence so remarkable it's alarming to mere mortals. He will always be found in dreary Victorian England. He will always solve the case.

If you think you want to avoid the complications of creating an arc for your protagonist by creating such a series, do so at your own risk. Yes, some of these series become best-selling franchises. So where's the risk?

Sir Arthur Conan Doyle grew sick of his commercial creation and notoriously launched Holmes off Reichenbach Falls to be rid of him. The public outcry ran the gamut from young men wearing black armbands to mourn the loss of Holmes to *The Strand Magazine* reportedly losing 20,000 subscribers after the story's publication in December 1893. Doyle wrote in his autobiography, "I have been much blamed for doing that gentleman to death, but I hold that it was not murder, but justifiable homicide in self-defense, since, if I had not killed him, he would certainly have killed me."

A writer with a successful mystery series came to one of my classes as a guest speaker while I was an MFA student. She had a good number of books out and a good many fans. After writing all those books to specifications her fans knew and enjoyed so well, she was eager to take her character and plots in new, darker directions. Her publisher wouldn't allow it, because it might upset the fan base.

Readers can take as much or as little time as they like between books. They can read other material between your stories. You, the writer, however, spend many hours of your day, months on end, to create each book ready to reach those eager hands. You do not get a break from your creations the way your readers do.

If you don't think you'll get bored and long to one day stretch your creative muscles, or if you don't think readers will ever tire of your particular storyline, by all means, write an arc-less protagonist. You may publish the next great literary franchise. But you may one day find yourself committing "justifiable homicide in self-defense."

YOUR ARC, YOUR THEME, YOUR CHARACTER, THE HEART OF YOUR STORY

We've touched on theme and its importance several times already, while discussing character flaws, motivation, and subplots. Now we're going even deeper by exploring how your character arc and your theme work together to pump blood through the heart of your story.

If you begin writing a book without identifying your major theme, you'll probably draft a meandering, unfocused story. Identifying your theme now, as part of your character development prewriting, will help you write a strong first draft.

Themes can, and do, emerge organically from the character. You can identify your character's issues, and then discover your themes. You can also identify your themes, and use them to shape some of your character's issues. If you want to write a story about father-son relationships, your character will need to be a son and possibly a father as well. You'll want to write some strife in those relationships, challenges your character needs to confront and overcome. Alternatively, you might not set out to write about father-son relationships, but by virtue of creating a father and a son in conflict you'll find that one of your themes is father-son relationships.

Let's revisit Steve, our high-powered criminal attorney. We've identified his flaws, and with them a number of plot points. How do those translate into workable themes? Steve is struggling to keep his family together without reducing his workload. His fatal flaw is hubris. Therefore, at the end of Steve's character arc, through the events of the plot, Steve needs to realize he can't do it all. He needs to accept help, whether from colleagues, a treatment program, his wife, or all of the above. Our theme could be the pressure a man feels to be successful in both the professional and the family arenas.

We could just as easily have chosen our theme first, then discovered Steve's fatal flaw and crafted a plot that dramatizes our theme. The choice, and the *tabula rasa*, is yours.

When you identify the theme of your story, you will know the crux of your character's arc, and vice versa.

Theme is a major element of any story, especially the character arc. Since you know about your character's fatal flaw, the relationships in his life, the subplots that have grown out of his relationships with supporting characters, and how you expect your character to be different at the end of the book than at the beginning, you know more than enough to identify your major theme.

Stories can, and normally do, contain more than one theme. As you write, minor themes may suggest themselves. For example, the theme I am exploring with Jess's character arc in The Skoghall Mystery Series is that of creating an independent and fulfilling life. Because my first book involves veterans with PTSD from two different eras, I've had readers ask me if each of my books will be focused on a social issue. It was not my intention to write about PTSD or veterans' issues, but those themes certainly emerged from my plot. The second book doesn't deal as explicitly with a social issue, but I do have a character who is a minority from an immigrant family serving in the sheriff's department. I have a service dog as well. And some of this book's events are setting me up for a further exploration of psychological trauma in the third book.

ONE STORY, TWO ARCS

When I talk with writers, one of the first things I ask them to do is describe their book's plot arc to me. "Give me a summary of what happens in the book from front cover to back cover," I say. It's surprising how many writers begin by telling me about the theme of the book. Without realizing it, they get right into the character arc. "That's great, and very important, but it's all theme," I say. "Now tell me the *plot*—how you show that on the page with events, action, the stuff that's happening."

Hearing about theme when I've asked for plot is not surprising. Your character arc and your plot arc are intrinsically entwined. They're like two parts of a whole, pieces of a pie, strands of a braid, the warp and woof... Let's take a closer look at how character arc and plot arc work together in your story.

> Theme is the stuff of the character arc and is distinct from plot. Plot is the dramatization of a story, including its themes, through action.

This repeated conversation has shown me that lots of writers set out to write a story about a broad concept, what it means to be a good father, for instance. From the concept, they discover the theme. Let's define theme again: *Theme* is the intangible something that your story is about, such as grief, love, power, or the cost of success. Theme defines the primary issues your character will struggle with over the course of the character arc. Theme is what makes your story distinct from other stories with similar plot elements, but theme and plot work together to craft a solid story.

Your book is *about* both its theme and its plot. When you focus on theme, you're focusing on your character's issues that will need to be resolved over the course of the character arc.

PERSONAL DEVELOPMENT, AND I DON'T MEAN ENROLL YOUR CHARACTER IN A KNITTING CLASS

Suppose your character is a toddler. The plot might involve potty training—that's an action with easily defined, tangible goals and obstacles. When the goal is accomplished, your toddler has reached a new stage of personal development—no longer needing diapers equals a new level of independence and self-control that will serve him well for the rest of his life. In this simple example, you can see how the plot and theme are related. The plot and the character's goal is to become potty trained. The theme and resultant personal growth is to become independent.

People don't read for plot; they read for theme. Let's consider our toddler as reader. You might write a lovely little picture book about potty training. It identifies the components of the potty, makes toilet paper more appealing than you would have thought possible, and reminds parents to reward their toddler's success. Do you think the toddler will want to read that book? No, because the toddler doesn't care about the goal of potty training. If your picture book includes a little boy or girl who smiles and has fun on the potty, who is rewarded for going potty, and who celebrates in his or her new big kid pants at the end of the story, then you'll have a book the toddler will want to read. Why? Because the theme of the book is appealing to the toddler, that is the joy of success and independence (no more diapers). That theme is related to and illustrated by the character arc, not the plot arc.

> We don't relate to the potty.
> We relate to the toddler.

The character pursues his *goal* through the plot arc. The character experiences *personal development* through the character arc. The character probably won't be aware of his own development through the character arc, but the writer must be aware so that the reader can experience the character's growth.

HOW TO DISTINGUISH
THEME FROM PLOT

We can't sit down and read an entire novel together, so we'll do the next best thing. We'll analyze a book's description.

Let me tell you about *A Stone's Throw*.

A Stone's Throw is about Simona, Gemma, and Peter. Simona and Gemma live an ocean apart and never meet, but they both love Peter. Simona paints a mural and the people she paints come to life. Gemma is dealing with depression. She's helped when, through a series of visions, she experiences the mural coming to life.

A Stone's Throw is also about longing, the act of creation, and the ways we lose and sometimes find ourselves.

The first description reveals events that occur in the plot. The second description reveals theme, which is all about the characters' arcs. You can consider the arc psychological, emotional, or spiritual, but the changes are internal and ultimately affect the characters' being.

When someone asks you what your book is about or when you're writing your sales copy, try to merge the plot and theme into one artful description. Here's the sales copy for *A Stone's Throw*. As you read it, notice where plot is revealed and where theme is revealed.

Simona Casale is a Minneapolis painter with a successful career. She never knew her mother, and the last thing she wants is a baby. Being at a pivotal moment on her artistic path, it's a bad time to find out she's pregnant. Gemma Ledbetter, a London homemaker, is desperate for the baby she can't have.

Simona and Gemma live an ocean apart and never meet, yet they have much in common: art, longing, and a magic that changes both of their lives. And then there is Peter, the man they love. Magic, like any great act of creation, comes at a price...and one of them will have to pay.

Let's identify the thematic elements in that description. In the first paragraph we find out that Simona never knew her mother and Gemma is desperate for a baby, that's the longing. Also, Simona is pregnant, so another theme is motherhood. The second paragraph names themes outright: art, longing, and magic. Peter is mentioned, so we discover the themes of love, love triangles, and love gained and lost. The final sentence mentions the act of creation, which is also a theme and refers to making art, making a baby, and reinventing yourself.

The themes become apparent in the plot elements. Theme must be dramatized through action on the page. Gemma trying to get pregnant is plot action; her longing for a baby is theme. Simona getting pregnant is plot action; her ambivalence about motherhood is theme. Peter's affair is plot action; love is theme.

Simona's and Gemma's character arcs are identified in this sentence: *A Stone's Throw* is about two women who never meet, one finding herself and one losing herself through a shared exploration of the relationship between motherhood and identity.

Plots are cheap. You can find the same plot elements in hundreds of stories, be they car crashes or shoot-outs or steamy kisses. It's the thematic material that distinguishes one steamy kiss from another. One reader might like stories about love triangles, but not women's identities. Another might not care about love triangles, but find women's identities a worthwhile topic. Character is the heart of your story and theme makes your character's arc unique.

Theme makes your story distinct from
other stories with similar plot elements.

EXERCISE 10: CONNECTING THEME, CHARACTER ARC, AND PLOT

In this exercise, you'll identify stories' themes from their descriptions and make the connection between theme, character arc, and plot. You might notice some commonalities within genres as well. For an example of the analysis of a book's description, refer to the description of *A Stone's Throw* above.

1. Go to an online bookseller and paste the sales copy from about twenty books into a word processing document. Choose books from multiple genres, including genres you don't read. Only pick from top-sellers so you know the copy is effectively moving readers to buy.

2. Now that you have many examples in one place, read them through with a couple of highlighters, one color for plot, another for theme.

3. Look at how theme and plot are woven together in the description.

4. What assumptions can you make about the main character's arc based on the thematic elements in the description?

5. Do you notice any patterns emerging? Commonalities within genres? What else did you notice?

6. Find several stories with similar plot elements. Compare the descriptions. What distinguishes those stories from each other? Which of those stories would you like to read, and why?

7. Note your discoveries in your journal.

This exercise is bordering on market research, so feel free to repeat this process when you're getting your own back cover copy ready, focusing this time on your specific genre.

GETTING THE ARC ON THE PAGE

Evolution is simply change. A character's arc defines the moments of your character's change along a chronology of events. The chronology of events are the vehicle for showing that change to your readers. *Showing* is using tangible actions on the page. If you think of the stage of the page, a tangible action is one an actor could perform that an audience could witness.

For example, this is telling: Another family dinner at his parents' house left him exhausted. This is showing: Arriving home from another dinner at his parents' house, he left his shoes at the door and went straight to the liquor cabinet to pour himself a double.

Suppose one of your themes is "allowing yourself to be loved." How would you show a reader that your character is evolving into someone who can let herself be loved? To begin with, you need to show her being guarded, distant, aloof, wary, or whatever combination of those works for your character. Maybe she receives a note from a boy and responds in the most embarrassingly romantic way possible, only to find out the note was a prank and now the mean girls are spreading rumors and everyone is laughing at her. She puts up walls to protect herself. Something will have to happen to get your character to open up and take a risk. Maybe she gets a note that is real and she assumes it's another cruel joke. And then, just before the boy gives up on her forever, she realizes she'll never know love if she isn't willing to let someone in. To show the reader this realization, put it into tangible action on the page. As the boy is leaving town, the girl rushes to the train station to tell him she loves him. She makes a grand gesture, perhaps recording a video of herself talking about how she feels, and in an act of courage and faith, she puts it in his hands to keep or share with the world as he will. There are thousands of possibilities.

```
Do not create a scene around what
    your character thinks or feels.
Create a scene around what she does.
Meaningful action is doable action.
```

In Sonja L. Perrin's science fiction novel, *Synthesis,* Shayne is a tomboy with plenty of emotional walls. She finds herself having feelings for the most unlikely partner on the planet, the Commander, a machine-man hybrid. She makes a daring move to express her attraction. Perrin shows her evolution in this scene by dramatizing the moment of change with tangible action.

> Our second kiss sent sparks relaying through my body. The world began to slip off its axis.
>
> Lightheaded, I broke the connection.
>
> He searched my face. "Am I doing something wrong?"
>
> "No." I breathed. "It's just that I...I'm not sure how..." I fell silent, flustered from the lack of air in the cavern.
>
> He looked human. Brow taut, sculpted muscles strained. Utterly human. Just dipped in graphene was all.

It didn't matter. Machine, man, whatever, I wanted him.

In a moment of hormone-laced daring, I shoved myself up and let his cloak fall to my waist.

He stared. Stunned, I think.

Nervous, I watched his eyes roam, literally map the topography of my body, right down to the scars and birthmarks.

I'd never been naked with a man, never felt this completely vulnerable. Not that there weren't opportunities. The timing—the boys—hadn't been right. The Commander was silent, still processing. Doubt twisted my stomach, mocking me. Had I misjudged the moment? Could he interpret the invitation? Was he even capable of reciprocating it?

Oh, Providence!

"I'm sorry." Humiliation flamed my cheeks. I grabbed the ends of the cloak ready to take refuge in it, but his hands enveloped mine.

"Please, do not cover up." There was sincere urgency in his expression, in the strength of his grasp. "I have performed a detailed risk analysis and am overriding conduct protocols. Please allow me to continue."

I nodded, nervous.

A moment later, he smiled. "There. It is done." The smile wavered. "Are you all right? You're shivering."

I couldn't answer. A gamut of emotions whirled inside me: Elation, desire, panic. Words were impossible.

"May I adjust the cloak?"

A small nod—all I could manage.

His hands gently tugged the rest of the material out from under me and in the process tipped me forward. I braced my palms on his chest, his skin like hot wax against my body.

His eyes brightened. I laughed.

The reader witnesses Shayne's actions and empathizes with her vulnerability and need. The reader understands—through empathy, not intellect—that Shayne is evolving as a person in this very moment. When we witness such a change, whether in each other or in a character, we respond. We are changed. That is the power of the character arc.

Find out about Sonja L. Perrin at the back of this book.

J.K. Rowling's Harry Potter series provides an excellent example of the character arc coming to fruition at the end of a long series. The first book opens with Harry as an orphan, sleeping in the cupboard under the stairs. His sleeping situation is tangible action on the page that shows the readers his miserable situation and what it means for Harry to not have loving parents. Over the course of the series, all of the father figures in his life end up dead: Black, Dumbledore, Lupin, and Snape. At the end of the final book, in the resolution, Rowling shows readers that Harry is grown up. He is married to Ginny and they have children. The resolution of Harry's character arc is that he now has a family to love, and they love him. Instead of missing his father and searching for a father figure, he has grown up and *is* a father. Rowling does not tell us this in narrative. She *shows* the reader in scene.

Character Arc for
Gemma of *A Stone's Throw*

Character
Evolution

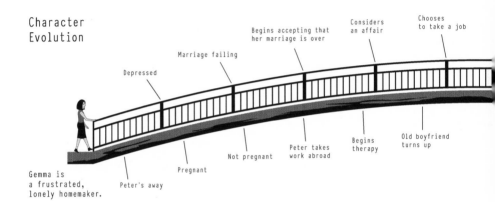

Plot Events

CHAPTER 9 : GOT ARC?

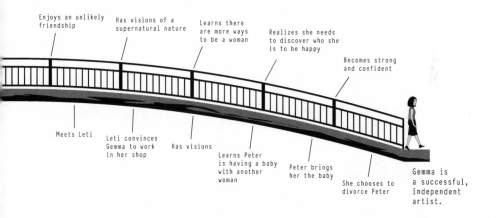

Enjoys an unlikely friendship

Has visions of a supernatural nature

Learns there are more ways to be a woman

Realizes she needs to discover who she is to be happy

Becomes strong and confident

Meets Leti

Leti convinces Gemma to work in her shop

Has visions

Learns Peter is having a baby with another woman

Peter brings her the baby

She chooses to divorce Peter

Gemma is a successful, independent artist.

The character arc defines the character's evolution over the course of the book or series. The arc's fruition, that is how the character is a different person at the end of the book than she was at the beginning, must be shown in tangible action in the resolution of the book or series, after the climax.

EXERCISE 11: THE SHAPE OF YOUR ARC IS ARC-LIKE

I like to draw things out. It's a useful way to see the relationship between the many, often complicated elements of a story. Novels are long, and I've bought a roll of paper meant for a child's art easel just so I could fit the entire story's arc on a single stretch of paper. I've also taped together sheets of printer paper to create the continuous line of my story's arc. Do what you have to do.

The example above is a reproduction of my hand-drawn character arc for Gemma of *A Stone's Throw*. Use it as a model for this exercise, which will help you create your character's arc. The instructions explain what you see in Gemma's arc.

1. On a large sheet of paper, draw an arcing line from left to right. This represents the character arc itself.

2.   Place a dot at the left end of the arc. Label it with a word or two that represent who your character is at the beginning of the book. "Gemma is a frustrated, lonely homemaker."

3.   Place a dot at the right end of the arc. Label it with a word or two that represent who your character is at the end of the book. "Gemma is a successful, independent artist."

4.   Along the top side of the arcing line, write words that define the evolutionary stages of your character. These words will largely describe emotional states of being or new abilities, like confidence or assertiveness, self-awareness or joy. This is more an art than a science, so don't get hung up on word choice. "Depressed. Marriage failing. Considers affair. Has visions."

5.   Along the bottom side of the arcing line, write words that represent actions and events that precipitate, facilitate, or illustrate the character's ongoing change. "Pregnant. Not pregnant. Old boyfriend turns up. Has visions. Peter brings her the baby."

When you're finished, the arc will map your character's evolution from front cover to back cover. By placing both evolutionary stages and plot points on the arc, you'll be able to see whether or not your character's change (top of the arc) is actually shown in tangible action on the page (bottom of the arc).

Why is this tangible action piece so critical? Because your reader is not in your head. Readers understand characters through the words on the page and nothing else is available to them. Couldn't you simply tell the reader that your character is a new person? Not if you are writing a *story*.

RECAP

- The character arc is the evolution of the main character over the course of the story; every main character is a different person at the end of the story than she was at the beginning.

- By identifying the theme of a story, you know the crux of the character arc, the personal journey the character must take and the personal conflict he must resolve at the end of the story.

- Readers relate to characters and their personal struggles: the story's theme, not the story's plot.

- As your character works her way through the plot events, she will experience personal development, thereby resolving the story's theme.

- Exercise 10: Connecting Theme, Character Arc, and Plot. You examine book descriptions to become familiar with the way theme is a critical component of story that entices readers to pick up a book. The exercise also shows you how theme and plot elements work together to shape a story, and that if you can identify a story's theme, you can identify the main character's arc.

- In a series, the character arc will span the series. There must be progress and a resolution of each book's themes along the way, but the overarching theme and arc will resolve in the final book of the series.

- The character's evolution must be dramatized on the page in tangible action in order to show it to the reader.

- Exercise 11: The Shape of Your Arc is Arc-Like. In this exercise, you draw your character's arc, visually tracking her evolution over the course of your story. Adding plot points to the arc ensures your character's evolution is playing out on the page in tangible action.

Chapter 10

The Big Uns

UNLIKABLE AND UNRELIABLE CHARACTERS

Unlikable characters and unreliable narrators are interesting to write, but they come with their own sets of challenges. Would you want to spend ten to twenty hours with someone you don't like? Or even six? Given how long it takes to read a novel, if you write an unlikable protagonist, you're asking a reader to spend a chunk of his free time with your unlikable character. Would you enjoy spending time with someone who lies to you? Well, maybe, if the story is *really* good.

DEFINING THE UNLIKABLE CHARACTER

You know that guy from work you don't like? Do you ever call him up and ask him to go hang out? No. And how come? Because you don't like him. An *unlikable* character is that guy.

Your point of view character is the vehicle for your story, our lens for viewing the world in which the story takes place, and if it's too uncomfortable a fit, if your character isn't likable, it's unlikely readers will want to finish your book.

Those characters people "love to hate" are not usually main characters, precisely because readers identify with the point of view character. Unlikable characters make great rivals, questionable friends, foils, and irritating presences in the main character's life. They do not make great main characters.

EXERCISE 12: UNLIKABLE CHARACTERS YOU KNOW

In this exercise, let's take a look at unlikable characters we already know.

1. Brainstorm all the unlikable characters you've encountered in books. Make a list.

2. Now star the ones who are point of view characters. How many are there?

3. Note how many characters are *truly* unlikable. A character can be a criminal genius and a loyal friend. Or a grouch who is somehow endearing. Or a cross old lady who softens once

someone shows her a little kindness. Does your list include characters with objectionable traits who are actually likable? If so, cross them off. They don't count, because they aren't really unlikable; they're just flawed humans, like the rest of us.

Note: You can give a cannibal a point of view, but you can't make him unlikable. I might not want to go dinner with him, but I have to enjoy his company enough to stick with the story.

4. See how many characters are unlikable, but in the end turn out to be good guys. Professor Snape, of J.K. Rowling's Harry Potter series, is a perfect example of this. Cross them off your list, too.
5. That leaves unlikable characters who are bad guys on the list. That's probably most of your list—probably all of it.
6. Do you have any unlikable protagonists?

I can think of only one: Brett Easton Ellis's Patrick Bateman, the first person narrator and antihero of *American Psycho*. It's the most uncomfortable book I've ever read. Bateman is a character I despise, and I hated every minute in his head—from the boring list of skin care products he uses to his discourse on Huey Lewis and the News to his despicable sex crimes. Ellis expected far too much of me as a reader. I read it because I assigned the book in a class on monsters in literature, otherwise I never would have finished it. So why did the book yield Ellis literary stardom? I could argue it was timely, experimental, and satirical. The book is a commentary on the young, wealthy, superficial, materialistic American elite of the 1980s. Maybe people were ready to reflect on that by the time the book was published in 1991.

When you think of other objectionable characters, like Humbert Humbert or Hannibal Lecter, you have to ask yourself if they are *truly* unlikable. They might be sleazy but charming, scary but fun, or criminal but brilliant. There is something about them that makes them appealing, despite their horrible qualities.

Write unlikable main characters at your own risk. It's unlikely readers will buy, finish, and recommend your book if you take on a truly unlikable protagonist.

HOW TO AVOID YOUR CHARACTER GETTING DUMPED

Other than assigning your book for a graduate seminar, why would a reader stick with an unlikable character? For one reason: fascination. That is the flip side of the character coin. Heads, he's likable, and tails, he's fascinating.

Your main character had better be likable *and* fascinating to fully engage a reader for a book-length story. And if he's not likable, you need to up the fascination factor exponentially to make up for his disagreeable personality and behavior.

Note that your point of view character could be a killer or a drunk, mentally ill or abusive, or simply buffeted by the Fates and still be likable. Having problems and doing bad (even unforgivable) things does not make a character unlikable. It may instead make him a *tragic hero*. The tragic hero evokes pity and fear, originating in Greek drama, such as Sophocles' *Oedipus the King*. Tom Ripley of Patricia Highsmith's *The Talented Mr. Ripley* is a tragic hero. He is deeply flawed, intentionally kills the only person who loves him, and yet he remains somehow likable. We pity him for the way his circumstances have forced his terrible choices, and we fear him for the ways in which he is like ourselves.

WRITING UNLIKABLE CHARACTERS

Unlikable characters can be fun to write and read. Here are some guidelines to help you create a character we love to hate.

- I don't recommend writing an unlikable protagonist, but as a primary or secondary character, he can greatly enrich the story. He might be the antagonist or a supporting character. Whether a good guy or bad guy, he can be the proverbial thorn in your protagonist's side.

- If you must write an unlikable protagonist, start with short experimental pieces and get some reactions from readers before you commit to writing a longer work.

- In a multiple point of view story, it is possible to create an unlikable point of view character who is either one protagonist or the antagonist. Having other point of view characters will buffer the reader from spending too much time inside that objectionable perspective.

- Make sure you understand why your character is unlikable: Wounds? Insecurities? Lack of a conscience? Trying too hard? Shallow? Use the source of the character's unlikable qualities to make her complex and real. Readers will be more patient and understanding with an unlikable character who is at least somewhat sympathetic.

- Follow your readers' lead. If you have an unlikable supporting character that readers love, make him the unlikable protagonist of a spin-off novella to see if readers love him enough to stick with him for a hundred pages. If they do, run with it.
- Make certain the unlikable supporting character's parts relate to the main character and main plot. Nothing extraneous. Nothing *just* for fun.
- Have fun with the unlikable character. Comedies are full of these types—we wouldn't want him in our lives, but we love to watch him rub the likable protagonist the wrong way!

LET ME TELL YOU A LIE

You've heard the old saying: There's his story. There's her story. And then there's the truth. We might read his story or her story, and both could be completely reliable. We read story to live someone else's experiences. That's why it's called a point of view and not a point of fact. But if he narrates *her* story, he might become an unreliable narrator, manipulating the truth to place blame, for example.

An *unreliable narrator* is lying *to the reader.* That means you, as author, need to place clues, inconsistencies in the story, that show the reader the story is being manipulated by an unreliable narrator. In other words, you *want* the reader to mistrust the narrator. To create an unreliable narrator, the reader must suspect she's being lied to, and that must be relevant to the story.

> An unreliable narrator is one we can't trust to tell us the truth.

WHAT MAKES A NARRATOR LIE?

A narrator might lie for the same reasons any of us might: guilt, shame, manipulation, greed, mental illness, memory loss, head trauma, unbearable grief, fun and games, ignorance of the truth...

A character can lie within the story to as many other characters as he wants to without being an unreliable narrator. An unreliable narrator is the character the *reader* ultimately cannot trust. Figuring that out, and then trying to figure out the real story, is part of the fun of following an unreliable narrator.

When working with an unreliable narrator, you are essentially constructing a mystery. The reader has to be shown clues that indicate the story is not all coming together. The reader at some point has to be able to make sense of the story, piecing together the truth around the version of the story the narrator has told the reader.

Dennis Lehane's *Shutter Island* provides an excellent example of an unreliable narrator. This is the story of a cop called to an island for the criminally insane to investigate the disappearance of a woman. The woman can't be found, dead or alive. As the mystery thickens, the cop has strange visions of drowned children. There's a conspiracy, a Nazi doctor, a storm trapping them on the island, inmates running amok, and things are not quite adding up. In the final twist, we learn that the cop's badge and gun are fakes. His partner is one of the doctors. He is, in fact, an inmate of Shutter Island. A doctor with revolutionary ideas hoped they could break through his psychosis and heal him by enacting his delusion.

The story is all a lie. We believe it because it's presented as the truth, and for the narrator, it is the truth. At some point, if we're paying attention, things don't add up and we start to doubt the narrator. Trying to figure out what's going on is part of the fun. We're deep into the mystery with the cop, wondering about the children, that missing woman, and of course the Nazi doctor. At the end, our hero, the brave cop, is another tragic hero. He's been lying to himself and therefore to us the entire time. Why? Because he can't face his grief, and he's built a massive, complicated delusion. The story we enter is his delusion.

The moment we realize the story is a lie is a wonderful twist. *The twist* is a moment of shocking realization when what we thought we knew is suddenly turned around and given new meaning.

WRITING AN UNRELIABLE NARRATOR

Unreliable narrators, like unlikable characters, can be fun to write and read. They add layers of complexity to a story by necessitating a mystery or a story within the story. Here are some guidelines to help you find the story that unreliable narrator is hiding.

- An unreliable narrator requires careful plotting. You'll have to keep track of two stories as you write, the truth and the lie, and you'll have to manage their presentation to the reader, building intrigue and avoiding confusion.

- An unreliable narrator could be the point of view character, in which case, the point of view would be written in the first person or the close third. If your narrative voice is too distant from the point of view character's perspective, you'll provide too much of the picture outside of that character's head to create unreliability. I'll discuss the various points of view in the point of view book. For now, it's enough to say that the reader experiences the story through the perspective of your point of view characters. The closer the point of view, the more restricted the reader's experience of the story is to that of the character.

- The unreliable narrator could also be a narrator external to the point of view character, in which case more distance would be appropriate, even required, to create the effect of unreliability.

- To write a character who lies to the reader, you'll need to craft a tight story. Sloppy execution will create confusion. An unreliable narrator is constructing a mystery around the question, "What really happened?"

- The story could end with a big reveal, the moment the reader realizes she's been lied to and pieces together the truth.

- The story could also leave the reader with an *ambiguous ending*, which is an open-ended and often uncomfortable ending. In which case, the reader has the sense things are not quite right with the narrator and can construct an alternate version of the story from the clues, but the narrator's lies are left intact.

- As with the unlikable character, the unreliable narrator presents certain challenges, so start with short experimental pieces to hone your skills before launching a novel with an unreliable narrator.

EXERCISE 13: THE FLIMFLAM MAN

Do this exercise any time you're considering writing an unreliable narrator. It will help you decide if an unreliable narrator is going to work for your story.

1. How is an unreliable narrator essential to your story?
2. Answer some questions about your narrator.
   - What does the narrator have to hide?
   - Is the narrator lying to himself, as well as the reader?
   - Why is the narrator compelled to lie?
   - What does he gain?
3. How will those lies fit into your plot? Consider their purpose in the story and what clues you'll leave the reader along the way.
4. How will your character's lies affect other characters?
5. Will you leave the reader uncertain at the end of the book or include a reveal in which all is made clear? Why?

If answering these questions makes the way to writing your story seem muddy instead of clear, reconsider using an unreliable narrator. If, on the other hand, your answers have motivated you to get writing, get writing!

RECAP

Unlikable and unreliable characters are challenging to write and can be challenging to read as well. Approach them with caution. As with anything in writing, if you're compelled or inspired to write one, be aware of the challenges inherent in the task and have fun with it.

- Unlikable characters make great antagonists and foils for your protagonist. They can be a source of irritation or comedic relief.
- An unlikable protagonist is difficult to write and read, because nobody wants to spend that much time with an unlikable person.
- To make an unlikable protagonist readable, ramp up the fascination factor.
- Exercise 12: Unlikable Characters You Know. This exercise helps you survey stories you've read for examples of truly unlikable protagonists.
- Unreliable narrators lie to the reader. The lie becomes part of the story and a mystery for the reader to solve.
- As writer, you need to plant clues for the reader that will help her discover the lies.

- You need to understand why your narrator lies to craft a cohesive, believable story.
- A story with an unreliable narrator can end with a twist, in which all is revealed, or be left ambiguous, in which case the reader must decide what the truth is.
- Exercise 13: The Flimflam Man. You analyze if and how an unreliable narrator will work for your story.

Chapter 11

Problems with Character (And How to Fix Them)

This chapter is a reference section to help you quickly identify and solve some of the big problems.

1. ZZZZZZZ

Is your character flat, dull, lacking that certain *je ne sais quoi*? In other words, is your character boring?

The Fix:

Make a list of everything you like about your character. Then make a list of your character's more questionable traits, the things that make him interesting and complicated. Is the second list full or skimpy? Is it interesting or flat? You might need to mix up your character's traits and personality to make him into someone readers can picture and understand.

And speaking of the page, are the traits you list being shown to the reader in tangible action on the page? Go through the manuscript with a highlighter and check your work. You might have great details in your head, but the reader will never discover your full character if you don't get those details on the page.

For more help, revisit chapters 2, The Heart of Your Story, and 3, Character Traits.

2. The Golden Boy

This is when your main character is too perfect, too kind, too pleasant. We all have flaws, and you need to ask yourself, "What's his problem?"

I know I'm practically perfect in every way, but I also have a couple of exes who could give you a very short...kind of short...a little long...list of my flaws.

The Fix:

When you don't know what makes your point of view character flawed, connect with his ex. He must have one somewhere in his backstory. Grab a journal and ask the ex, "What led up to your breakup?" See what comes. (This is a freewriting exercise. See Exercise 3 if you need instructions.)

After you discover what led to their breakup, ask the ex, "What were his bad habits?" or "How did he disappoint you?" or "What are his flaws?"

You might be surprised by what you discover about your main character when you get out of his head and "talk" to someone who knows him intimately, who probably knows things he doesn't know about himself. Keep going until you have the material you need to take the halo off your character.

For more help, revisit chapter 4, Flaws.

3. Backstory Bog-Down

If your backstory is clogging the pipes and slowing the flow of your action, you've got too much of a good thing, or it's in the wrong place, or you're using the wrong method of revealing backstory.

The Fix:

First, ask yourself if you're front-loading information. This often happens at the beginning of the book, but it could happen at the start of a chapter or scene as well. Do not frontload information to set up your story. Let the story unfold naturally and place backstory only when and where it's relevant.

Second, make certain the information that you're revealing is relevant to the *now*-story. If it isn't related to what's going on right now in your character's life, cut it or move it elsewhere.

Third, consider how you are revealing the backstory and how that affects the pace of the whole. Also ask if you're revealing too much or trying to keep something off the page that can't be kept out of a scene without creating a hole in the scene. Review the methods for writing backstory: narrative exposition, flashback, and dialogue. If your backstory is relevant and properly placed but still feels like it's bogging down the action, try using one of the other methods of revealing backstory.

For more help, revisit chapter 5, History and Backstory.

4. Carried by the Current

If your character is passive, she's not driving the story the way she should be. This occurs when things *happen to* your character. Manifest destiny is a fine way to launch a hero's journey, but once begun, your hero must employ free will.

The Fix:

Present your character with situations that require she make a choice. Give her repercussions that lead her to make a new choice.

It's possible you feel like you're constantly responding to circumstances. That is the stuff of life. Most of it is mundane. Dull. Boring. And that is why you're writing fiction: to introduce us to your intriguing character, the one who transcends the mundane.

There are reasons why the villain kidnaps, the victim is kidnapped, and the hero rescues. Give your hero agency. Don't tie her hands.

For more help, revisit chapter 6, Agency.

5. The Couch Potato

The problem with characters who lack motivation isn't that they sit around doing nothing, it's that what they do doesn't really make sense to the reader. Your character's actions should be compelled and compelling.

The Fix:

When your character does something, ask yourself why she does it. Write down the answer. Then ask again. Answer again. Keep going until you've exhausted answers. Then look at your paper. Are the answers compelling? Do they make sense to you? Is that action the only action your character could take that feels inevitable? If you don't answer yes to each of those questions, go back to the beginning. Examine your character's traits and backstory until you come up with a more compelling source of motivation for your character.

For Jess in *The Murder in Skoghall,* I had to ask why she stays in a haunted house. Because she sunk all of her money into it. Because she just uprooted herself and moved to a new town. She doesn't want to fail. Because she fell in love with her house. Because she just went through a divorce and the idea of "home" is extremely compelling for her right now. Because more than anything, she wants to be an artist in an arts community. Because she's a fighter. Because she's incredibly empathetic and feels sorry for Bonnie. Because this is her chance to start over and live the life she's always wanted. Because she's alone for the first time in her life and she has to prove to herself she can hack it.

Once you have your list of answers, note that they are all true for your character. The intangible, deeper motivations are the more compelling. They're the reasons your character will stay in the game through the climax.

Is your list of answers compelling enough to keep your character invested as the stakes rise?

For more help, revisit chapter 7, Motivation.

6. The Dreaded Soggy Middle

If you aren't working with your supporting characters and your subplots, you might find your plot has slowed down in the middle and your readers are yawning. This is a character problem disguised as a plot problem.

The Fix:

Get mean! Writers like their main characters. It's that empathy thing that goes with being human. Just like you wouldn't want to cause your child or partner pain, you hate to hurt that character you birthed from your imagination, like Venus from the sea.

Fiction is bad things happening to interesting people. Your mantra should be "From the fry pan to the fire." When in doubt, ask yourself, "How could this get worse?" Write that.

Another Fix:

It's possible that you think you're doing all kinds of horrible things to your character, but the stakes aren't high enough. For stakes to be high, they have to be personal.

If your character sees some random car run over her neighbor's dog, she'll feel bad for the dog and the neighbor. If your character runs over the neighbor's dog, she has "skin in the game," that is, *stakes.* Now she's a dog killer. She'll probably feel guilt and remorse. Her relationship with her neighbor is threatened. She might have to pay emergency vet bills she can't afford.

The difference between those two scenarios is that the witness doesn't have to suffer any repercussions from the event, while the participant has to suffer several.

A Third Fix:

It's also possible that you have the right event occurring at the right time in the story, but your character is slinking off alone to be depressed. You aren't going to rub salt into your own wound, and neither is your character! When you need him to get back in the game, use other characters to make his situation worse.

Most of us have many relationships in our lives. Your character needs to have several on the page: spouse, parents, children, bosses, employees, the delivery driver...

Suppose your character just lost his job. He goes home and before he can tell his wife about being laid off—or worse, getting fired—his son rushes to the door to tell him about the gaming system he wants. What will your character do? Yell at his kid? Pour a drink without a word to anyone? Make a promise he can't keep?

The event, getting fired, hasn't changed, but its impact on your character is compounded by the reactions of others in his life. Maybe he felt angry when he left work, but now he feels shame. Getting fired threatens his financial stability. As soon as he interacts with others, his identity as a provider is threatened. Now his relationships are threatened as well.

For more help, revisit chapter 8, Supporting Characters.

7. Your Character Fails to Evolve

If your character isn't noticeably different at the end of the book or series than she was at the beginning, you're missing a character arc.

The Fix:

Answer this: How is your character different at the end of the book than at the beginning? If you can't pinpoint the change in your character, look at the story as a whole. What is the theme of your story? Your character's arc is closely connected to your theme. If the theme is father-son relationships, your character might be an angry son at the beginning of the story and an appreciative son at the end. If your theme is freedom, your character might be living a constricted life at the beginning of your story, and living a life of her choosing at the end of it.

If you know exactly how your character has evolved, but your beta readers don't, you need to look at the resolution of the story, the part that follows the climax. Show in tangible action on the page that your character's evolution has come to fruition. Do that by writing a scene that illustrates your character's change. Don't tell us your character has overcome a fear of heights; show her atop a mountain. Don't tell us your character has overcome his commitment phobia; show him popping the question. Don't tell us your character has achieved freedom from addiction, show him receiving his one-year clean and sober medallion.

For more help, revisit chapter 9, Character Arc.

8. Avoid the Heartbreaking Breakup

Part of being likable is being relatable. Human beings are hardwired for empathy, and readers want to live your story vicariously through your character. If a reader dumps your character, it's because the character is a poor fit for the reader, just like in relationships.

The Fix:

The two sides of the character coin are likable and fascinating. You need to up your character's likability and fascination factors. Remember, the less likable your character, the more fascinating he must be to warrant your reader's interest.

Another Fix:

If you're certain your character is likable and fascinating, but readers aren't getting her, pull out your highlighter again. Mark scenes where you *show* on the page that your character has the qualities you've assigned her. The reader can only judge your character by what is *on the page*.

A Third Fix:

It's possible that you want your protagonist to be unlikable. In that case, identify his redeeming quality. For example, he might be an antisocial drug addict with a superiority complex, but he's brilliant. That redeeming quality, if properly developed and shown on the page will keep readers engaged, even with an otherwise repellant character.

For more help, revisit chapter 10, Unlikable Characters.

9. Other

Are you having a problem with character that wasn't covered in this book? Visit www.WordEssential.com/JoinStoryWorks and join the mailing list. Let me know what's troubling you, and I'll do my best to answer your question in an upcoming newsletter.

Now that you've read *The Story Works Guide to Writing Character*, and have completed all the exercises, you know how to create a memorable character your readers will love—or love to hate.

It begins with an idea for a story and ends with a notebook full of specific details that add up to a person with a past, who's willing to jump in and take action, who suffers the consequences all along the way to the kind of realization that leads to satisfying change. That might not sound easy, but it shouldn't sound hard—not any more. Like so many things worth doing, it's simply a process.

Now, go have fun with the *tabula rasa* and all of your wonderful creations!

Get Your Bonus

Thank you for reading *The Story Works Guide to Writing Character!*

Get three special episodes of the Story Works Round Table. In these video conversations about craft, Alida and her co-hosts, Kathryn and Matt, discuss character traits (chapter 3), history and backstory (chapter 5), and motivation (chapter 7).

www.WordEssential.com/StoryWorksCharacterBonus

While you're at the site, don't forget to join the mailing list.
www.WordEssential.com/JoinStoryWorks

You'll receive a downloadable, fillable Agency Tree worksheet (chapter 6), with instructions and a new example, to help you keep your characters in the game.

You'll also:

- receive Alida's newsletter with videos of writing tips,
- catch each new episode of the Story Works Round Table when it's released,
- be notified when future books in The Story Works Guide to Writing Fiction Series come out,
- be the first to hear about writing courses, and
- get special offers.

Don't forget the cool factor!

Acknowledgments

I feel incredibly blessed to do what I do and am grateful to the many wonderful people in my life, especially my editing and coaching clients.

One of those clients was Chris Fox, who wrote the foreword to this book. Last fall, we were wrapping up a coaching call and he said, "So when are you going to write your craft book?" I had been thinking about writing "my craft book" for some time, but it hardly seemed urgent and it was, along with other books of mine, seated on the back burner. Chris said, "Because I want to read it." Those words bumped this project from back burner to front. I doubt Chris realizes what an impact his casual inquiry has had on my life, but this book would not be in your hands this year (and I don't know how long it would have taken) had he not asked me about my craft book.

At the beginning of this journey, I put out a call for an apprentice, someone who would "work to learn." I wanted someone to help with organizational tasks to free me up to write the books, and was surprised and delighted by the number of people willing to put in a little time helping me in order to further their understanding of story craft. I wound up with not one, but two apprentices. Kathryn Arnold and Matt Herron are the best teammates I could hope for, each bringing valuable knowledge and skills to the table, from organizational prowess to website development. We were having so much fun talking craft during our regular calls that we created the Story Works Round Table, a video series of conversations about story craft. You can find those at www.WordEssential.com/StoryWorksRoundTable. I owe massive thanks to Kathryn and Matt for all of their assistance so far and am very excited about our ongoing collaboration at the Story Works Round Table.

Bryan Cohen, Chris Fox, Robert Scanlon, and Simon Whistler have been constant sources of support and feedback, without which I fear I would be half as far in twice the time. Whenever I need it, they provide nudges, shoves, hard-ass deadlines, and the terrifying Cohen Glower. Thank you, guys. I am so very happy to count you among my friends.

To all of my editing and coaching clients who gave me permission to excerpt your work, thank you for your faith in me. If you don't appear in Character, we have four more books to go!

To Sonja L. Perrin, M.A. Robbins, D.J. Schuette, and Judy K. Walker, whose works are excerpted in this book, I am truly grateful for your contribution to this discussion of character. Your wonderful words are now helping other writers develop their craft.

The care and expertise of Daria Brennan, Jana Rade, and Dara Syrkin was invaluable as I turned this project into a book ready to enter the world and the hands of readers. My thanks to each of you for sharing your gifts with me.

Contributing Writers

KATHRYN ARNOLD

Kathryn Arnold writes fantasy and anything else that sparks her creativity from her home in Kingston, Washington. She currently earns her living as an insurance underwriting assistant, where she also creates marketing and web copy. When not writing, she plays (and teaches) piano and keyboard in a band (or two), and is working on starting a ministry team with her husband. You can find Kathryn at www.SkyFireWords.com.

CHRIS FOX

Chris Fox has been writing since he was six years old and started inflicting his work on others at age eighteen. By age twenty-four, people stopped running away when he approached them with a new piece. Shortly thereafter, he published his first story in The Rifter. Chris lives in Novato California with his wife, where he writes several successful science fiction and speculative fiction series, as well as a popular nonfiction series for writers. You can find Chris at www.ChrisFoxWrites.com.

SONJA L. PERRIN

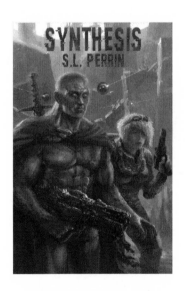

Sonja L. Perrin writes science fiction with a dash of romance. She lives in the High Desert in Southern California where tumbleweeds and Joshua trees abound. Whether researching artificial intelligence or untangling string theory, she is always plotting new and inventive ways to conquer galaxies not so far away. Sonja enjoys great books, tacos, and creamer flavored with coffee. She adores her husband and their two spoiled dogs, Latte and Brulee. You can find Sonja at www.SLPerrin.com.

M.A. ROBBINS

M.A. Robbins is the author of *The Tilt* post-apocalyptic action series. A long time Alaskan, he lives in Anchorage with his wife and their seventy-five pound chocolate lab puppy, TBone. He has a taste for unique characters, twisting plots, and homemade clam chowder. You can find Mike at www.MARobbins.com.

D.J. SCHUETTE

D.J. Schuette is an author and editor currently residing in the chilly suburbs of Minneapolis, Minnesota. His work covers a variety of genres, from dark thrillers to horror to YA fantasy. He is a published and award-winning songwriter and poet. His short story "The Nox" recently appeared in the second edition of *Creepy Campfire Quarterly*. Though to look at him it would seem all but impossible, D.J. has a lovely daughter and gorgeous wife. He is also the owner of quite possibly the most adorable dog on the planet. You can find D.J. at www.DJSchuette.com.

JUDY K. WALKER

Judy K. Walker is the author of the ongoing *Sydney Brennan Mysteries,* a private investigator series set in Tallahassee, Florida. She's currently also working on the thriller *Dead Hollow Trilogy,* set in a fictional Appalachian town nothing like the one she grew up in—she swears! She writes from rainy east Hawaii where she lives with her husband and their pack (three dogs, a troublemaking cat, and assorted geckos and sink frogs). If she's not tapping away at her computer, she hopes she's in her snorkel fins. You can find Judy at www.JudyKWalker.com.

About the Author

Alida Winternheimer entered this world holding a mechanical pencil and sheaf of loose-leaf paper—at least, it seems that way to her. The book she couldn't do without is a blank one. With unlimited pages. Always hungry for knowledge, she has a Master of Fine Arts in Writing from Hamline University and a Master of Liberal Studies from the University of Minnesota. She happily shares the knowledge she's acquired as your writing coach at Word Essential.

She writes several genres, from fairy tale to literary, and edits all genres. To date, she has published three novels and several short stories in literary journals, two of which were nominated for the Pushcart Prize. She is constantly thinking up new characters—living and dead—to inhabit her worlds.

She lives in the fabulous Minneapolis, Minnesota, with her golden retriever, Seva the Wonder Dog. When she's not writing, editing, or teaching, she facilitates Seva's career as a demonstration service dog, and likes to kayak or snowshoe, depending on the season. She also bikes, goes camping, feeds the animals, hugs the trees, and counts her lucky stars.

Please go to www.WordEssential.com/About to find more information about Alida and her work.

If you'd like to contact Alida, send her a note at Alida@WordEssential.com.

Glossary and Index

TERM	CHAPTER	PAGE	DEFINITION
Active protagonist	6	116	A main character who makes choices that shape the story. See also Agency and Passive protagonist
Agency	6	116	A character's ability to make choices and take actions that lead to specific consequences. See also Active protagonist and Passive protagonist.
Ambiguous ending	10	201	An open-ended conclusion to a story that leaves the reader to make a decision about the meaning or resolution of story events. Many readers find these endings uncomfortable.
Arc, character arc	9	169	The main character's internal change, or evolution, brought about by the events of the story. To have a complete arc, a character must be a different person at the end of the story than she was at the beginning. See also Flaw.

TERM	CHAPTER	PAGE	DEFINITION
Backstory	5	72	Backstory consists of parts of the character's past that a reader needs to learn to understand the plot.
			Backstory differs from history in that it must be included somewhere, somehow on the page so that the reader understands why your character behaves the way he does in the here and now.
			See also History.
Character	2	15	First, character is the vehicle through which a reader engages with a story.
			Second, character is any conscious being who acts in a story and changes over time.
Climax	3	32	The culminating event or incident in a story in which the main conflict reaches its zenith, and leads inevitably to the story's resolution.
Development	2	16	The process by which a character or other aspect of story is created or improved.
Dialogue	3	27	When a character speaks aloud. Dialogue is signaled to the reader by surrounding the line(s) with quotation marks. Dialogue tags attribute the spoken line(s) to the character who is speaking.

TERM	CHAPTER	PAGE	DEFINITION
Empathize/ Empathetic connection	2/9	15/170	The way in which a reader connects with a character on an emotional level. The reader's experience of living the story vicariously through the character. The means by which a reader is moved by a story.
Flashback	5	82	A scene in which character and reader goes back in time to show a character's backstory in scene. Transitions are made with signaling sentences that let the reader know that the narrative is now exploring past action.
Flaw and Fatal flaw	4	56-57	A flaw is anything your character is or does that is less than ideal and that affects the plot arc. A fatal flaw is a flaw that will destroy the character if he or she can't change. It is the crux of the character arc. See also Arc.
Genre	3	35	A category of fiction, such as science fiction, fantasy, romance, western, etc., that carries with it certain, specific reader expectations.

TERM	CHAPTER	PAGE	DEFINITION
Goal and obstacles	7	129	Goal is what your character wants. This can be a tangible or intangible goal, depending on whether it is a plot or character-related goal.
			Obstacles are what stand in the way of accomplishing the goal. These can be tangible or intangible obstacles, depending on whether they are plot or character-related obstacles.
			E.g. Plot related: Treasure - Dragon
			Character related: Prove worth to family - Fear
History	5	71	A character's life story. Everything that happened in the past that makes him who he is. History affects motivation.
			History differs from backstory in that it does not need to be included on the page for the reader to understand why your character behaves the way he does in the here and now.
			See also Backstory.
Hook	8	140	An open, or unresolved, question at the end of a chapter or book in a series that entices the reader to continue the story.

TERM	CHAPTER	PAGE	DEFINITION
In scene	3	42	When an action is shown "in scene," it is acted out by characters in real time in the now-story. It is shown, not told.
			When writing in scene, the writer is focused on showing characters' actions on the page, as opposed to shifting into narrative exposition, summary, or internal thoughts of the point of view character.
Inevitability	7	134	The sense that no matter how difficult or seemingly crazy the protagonist's choices, there is no true alternative. Inevitability ensures the plausibility of the story and credibility of the character. It pulls the character (and reader) through to the climax.
Intrigue	5	78	Questions the writer expects a reader to ask as she reads the story, because of the specific material on the page. E.g. If this character has anxiety around water, then the reader will wonder what happened to her involving water.
			Questions raised as intrigue are eventually addressed in a series of reveals or a big reveal.
			See also Reveal.

TERM	CHAPTER	PAGE	DEFINITION
Life lessons	3	33	Intangible lessons a character must learn over the course of the story that result in personal growth. E.g. Learning to trust someone is a life lesson. See also Arc.
Likable	4	63	A likable character is one the reader wants to spend time with, because the character is pleasant, enjoyable, relatable, sympathetic, and good company. If she's not all those things, she might be funny, exciting, or charismatic. Whatever her combination of traits, they are engaging, not repulsive. See also Unlikable.
Main Character	2	13	Also known as the protagonist or point of view character. Your main character is the heart of your story. The reader empathizes with this character and lives the story vicariously through her. See also Point of view.
Narrative exposition	5	80	Writing in your narrator's or authorial voice that creates mood, sets the scene, paints a picture, reflects, goes inside, and all those other things your busy point of view character isn't going to do or is doing quietly, internally.

TERM	CHAPTER	PAGE	DEFINITION
Nature and nurture	3	23	The internal qualities (nature) and external experiences (nurture) that form a person or character's identity. The writer's job is create a character who has been shaped by both nature and nurture. See also Tabula rasa.
Pacing	5	94	The speed at which events seem to be occurring within the story. The reader's experience of time within the story.
Passive protagonist	6	116	A main character that does not make choices or shape his own story. Stuff happens to and around him. See also Active protagonist and Agency.
Point of view	2	15	The perspective of the main character. The reader experiences the story through this character. Every story is shaped by the perspective from which it is told. See also Main character.
Primary characters	3	26	Supporting characters who are important to the plot. They are named and fully developed, with major roles in the protagonist's life. See also Secondary and Tertiary characters.

TERM	CHAPTER	PAGE	DEFINITION
Props	3	40	Short for properties. All the objects your character handles over the course of the story. Also decorations within the character's environment. Props help define a character's personality, such as style choices. Characters have relationships with these objects, such as the inherited vase he hates, but can't get rid of. Choose props carefully, because they help to define the character for the reader.
Qualities	3	32	Inherent aspects of your character, like personality traits. See also Nature and nurture, Skills, and Traits.
Resolution	9	169	The sense of completion and satisfaction at the end of a story. Resolution completes the character and plot arcs of your story.
Reveal	5	78	Transitive verb: the process of exposing information to the reader. Noun: The moment of "the reveal" when the writer answers questions the reader has been led to ask. These questions are referred to as intrigue. These answers are often found in a character's backstory. See also Intrigue.

TERM	CHAPTER	PAGE	DEFINITION
Role	3	30	Each character has a purpose within the story determined by the genre, plot, and her relationship to the protagonist. Ask what does this character have to do to fulfill this purpose? The answer will help shape the character.
			E.g. A character whose role it is to sail the seas will need different skills and traits than a character whose role it is to host dinner parties.
			See also Skills and Traits.
Secondary characters	3	28	Minor supporting roles in a story. These characters have names and dialogue, but aren't critical to the plot and aren't very important in the protagonist's life. A stable of disposable characters for the writer to use in the plot. Less well-developed than primary characters, they are often colorful additions to a scene.
			See also Primary and Tertiary characters.
Show/Showing	9	182	Using tangible action on the page. Think of the stage of the page, tangible action is one an actor could perform that an audience could witness.
			See also In scene and Tell/Telling.

TERM	CHAPTER	PAGE	DEFINITION
Skills	3	32	Skills are learned abilities that a character can utilize. They may have been picked up before the story began or during the story. See also Qualities and Traits.
Soggy middle	8	144	When characters do legwork or traveling necessary to a cohesive plot, but dull to read. During these passages, the tension drops and readers lose interest in the story.
Subplot	8	137	Narrative threads that showcase your character's life and the themes of your work. The plot is focused on action; subplots are focused on relationships.
Sympathetic/ sympathize	4	63	Feelings of pity or sorrow for another. The reader's experience of feeling bad for the characters' misfortunes. See also Empathy and Point of view.
Tabula rasa	3	23	The notion that a baby begins life as a "blank slate," popularized by the Victorians from the writings of philosopher John Locke. Every character begins as a blank slate and the writer's job is to create a whole, relatable being from nothing. See also Nature and nurture.

TERM	CHAPTER	PAGE	DEFINITION
Tell/Telling	5	89	A weak narrative style in which the writer talks about, explains things to, or slips into anecdotal writing. Telling creates flat, prose that fails to engage the reader's imagination. See also In scene and Show/Showing.
Tension, dramatic tension	8	142	What the reader feels when there is an unresolved question implied by the story, both through the action and the relationships on the page. As trouble increases for the character, the reader feels increasing concern over the outcome.
Tertiary characters	3	28	Extras and walk-on characters. They typically don't have a name and if they have dialogue, it's brief and unremarkable. See also Primary and Secondary characters.
Theme	4	69	The intangible something that your story is about, such as grief, love, power, or the cost of success. Theme defines the primary issues your character will struggle with over the course of the character arc. Theme is what makes your story distinct from other stories with similar plot elements. See also Arc.

TERM	CHAPTER	PAGE	DEFINITION
Tragic hero	10	196	A character whose arc ends in great suffering, destruction, or distress. The tragic hero evokes pity and fear, originating in Greek drama, such as Sophocles' Oedipus the King.
Traits	3	31	A character's distinguishing characteristics. The writer chooses these for the character, molding her to fit the writer's vision of the character as well as the demands of the story. See also Qualities and Skills.
Twist	10	200	A surprising change in the story that comes as a moment of shocking realization for the reader. What the reader thought they knew is suddenly given new meaning.
Unlikable	10	194	An unlikeable character is one a reader is not able to empathize or engage with. Readers will not want to spend time with him, because he is unpleasant or repulsive. Unlikable characters are most often primary or secondary characters. See also Likable.
Unreliable narrator	10	198	An unreliable narrator is one the reader can't trust to tell the truth. The writer places evidence within the story to create distrust between the reader and narrator.

TERM	CHAPTER	PAGE	DEFINITION
Verisimilitude	5	73	The appearance of being true or real. If a story (or a component of a story) has verisimilitude, the reader gets the impression that it "feels" true.
WWWWW+H	2	14	The five Ws plus the H of journalism: Who, What, When, Where, Why, and How. These are fundamental to both journalism and storytelling. Character = who and why Plot = what and how Setting = where and when

List of Exercises